Transport Prices and Costs in Africa

Transport Prices and Costs in Africa

A Review of the Main International Corridors

Supee Teravaninthorn
Gaël Raballand

THE WORLD BANK
Washington, DC

1818 H Street NW
Washington DC 20433
Telephone: 202-473-1000
Internet: www.worldbank.org
E-mail: feedback@worldbank.org

ISBN-13: 978-0-8213-7650-8
eISBN: 978-0-8213-7655-3
DOI: 10.1596/978-0-8213-7650-8

Library of Congress Cataloging-in-Publication Data

Teravaninthorn, Supee.
    Transport prices and costs in Africa : a review of the main international corridors / by Supee Teravaninthorn, Gaël Raballand.
        p. cm.
    Includes bibliographical references.
    1. Transportation—Africa—Costs. I. Raballand, Gaël. II. Title.
HE195.5.A35T47 2008
388'.049—dc22

                                                                           2008040248

Cover photo: Gaël Raballand, Washington DC, United States
Cover design: Candace Roberts, Quantum Think, Philadelphia, PA, United States

Contents

Foreword

One of the few things that African policy makers, development partners, civil society, and policy researchers agree on is that Africa has a serious infrastructure deficit. Only 25 percent of Africans have access to electricity. Less than 7 percent of arable land is irrigated. Two out of every three Africans lack access to sanitation. Only 65 percent have access to an improved water source. Perhaps the most compelling problem is that of road infrastructure. There are fewer kilometers of roads in Africa today than there were 30 years ago. Some 70 percent of Africa's rural population lives more than 2 km from an all-season road. And the cost of transporting goods in Africa is the highest in the world. Not only have high transport costs raised the cost of doing business, impeding private investment, but they serve as an additional barrier to African countries' benefiting from the rapid growth in world trade. Especially for Africa's many landlocked countries, high transport costs mean that, even if they liberalize their trade regimes, they will remain effectively landlocked.

While everyone agrees on the problem, there are different approaches to a solution. One view is that, if Africa has an infrastructure deficit, the solution is to plug that deficit by investing in infrastructure—build new roads, power plants, and irrigation canals. Another is to identify the causes of Africa's infrastructure deficit and address them directly. For if the problem is policy or institutional failures that prevent infrastructure from being productive—irrational power tariffs, weak regulations, inadequate operations, and poor maintenance—then simply building new infrastructure without addressing these problems will not improve the situation. Africa will still have an infrastructure deficit—but with higher debt.

This book is a contribution to the second approach. By examining the costs associated with transporting goods on four major corridors in four different parts of the continent, the authors derive a surprising result. Along these corridors, Africa's transportation costs are no higher than in other developing countries, such as China. But transportation *prices* are much higher. The difference is the set of informal payments and profits earned by trucking companies. The authors go on to show that the source of these high profit margins is the set of regulations in many African countries that restrict entry of new companies, enabling incumbents to earn large profits. They point to the example of Rwanda—a landlocked country that deregulated its transport sector and saw a dramatic drop in transport prices almost overnight.

Just as important as the findings of this book is the process by which it was prepared. Before publishing their results, the authors conducted extensive consultations with government officials, trucking companies, and civil society and policy analysts in Africa. We always have more confidence in the results when they have been vetted by the people on the ground. But there is another benefit to these consultations. If we are to effect change in Africa—to lower infrastructure costs so African firms can compete better in world markets—we will need reforms in the policy and regulatory arenas. These reforms are deeply political. Vested interests will resist them. The only way reform will occur is if the public is informed about the benefits—so politicians will see that it is in their interest to promote such reform. This book, and the way it was produced, is a major step in that direction.

Shantayanan Devarajan
Chief Economist, Africa Region
The World Bank
August 2008

Acknowledgments

The main authors of this paper are Supee Teravaninthorn and Gaël Raballand. Hernan Levy and Patricia Macchi contributed extensively to this book as well as Jean-François Marteau, Arnaud Desmarchelier, Monique Desthuis-Francis, Charles Kunaka, and Rodrigo Archondo-Callao. Ann May edited the paper, and Ann Njuguna supported the team. Salim Refas also contributed at the beginning of the task.

The authors would like to thank our peer reviewers who reviewed the paper throughout the research process: Aurelio Menendez, John Hine, Dino Merotto, and Baher El-Hifnawi. Their comments were always helpful.

Thanks also guidance from Sanjivi Rajasingham, resources from Mark Tomlinson, Vivien Foster, Amakoé Adoléhoumé, and friends and colleagues in the Africa Transport Unit (AFTTR) with whom we discussed the subject issues during our research period.

The authors wish to thank Jacqueline Meyo (from the Commission de la Communauté Economique et Monétaire de l'Afrique [CEMAC]), Jean-Kizito Kabanguka (from the Northern Corridor Transit Transport Coordination Authority [NCTTCA]), and Barney Curtis (from the Federation of East and Southern African Road Transport Associations [FESARTA]) for their help in organizing the stakeholder's workshops in Bangui, Kampala, and Pretoria.

The authors also thank the European Economic Community (EEC) group and especially Fares Khoury for having supervised and carried out, under contract, the trucking survey, which has provided important primary data for the study. Finally, the team is grateful to all the truckers and trucking companies that responded to the surveys and participants in the stakeholders' workshops in Ouagadougou, Bangui, Kampala, and Pretoria.

The findings and interpretations of this book are those of the authors. They do not represent the views of the World Bank, its executive directors, or the countries they represent. Any errors or imperfections that remain in the book are the authors'.

Abbreviations

AFTTR	Africa Transport Unit
APR	annual percentage rate
BARC	Bureau d'Áffrètement Routier Centrafricain
BGFT	Bureau de Gestion du Fret Terrestre
BNF	Bureau National de Fret
BRF	Bureau Régional de Fret
CAR	Central African Republic
CAS	Country Assistance Strategy
CBC	Conseil Burkinabé des Chargeurs
CEMAC	Commission de la Communauté Economique et Monétaire de l'Afrique
CNBRF	Centre National des Bureaux Regionaux de Fret
CNR	Comité National Routier
CNUT	Conseil Nigérien des Utilisateurs des Transports
CSIR	Council for Scientific and Industrial Research
DRC	Democratic Republic of Congo
EAC	East African Community
EEC	European Economic Community
ESW	economic and social work
EU	European Union
FCFA	Franc Communauté Financière Africaine

FESARTA	Federation of East and Southern African Road Transport Associations
GDP	gross domestic product
GTZ	Gesellschaft für Technische Zusammenarbeit
HDM-4	Highway Development and Maintenance Model 4
IEG	Independent Evaluation Group
IFS	International Financial Statistics
IMF	International Monetary Fund
km	kilometer
LPI	Logistics Performance Index
MFN	most favored nation
NCTTCA	Northern Corridor Transit Transport Coordination Authority
NTC	National Trade Corridor
OECD	Organisation for Economic Co-operation and Development
ONT	Office National du Transport
OTRAF	Organisation des Transporteurs Routiers du Faso
RED	Roads Economic Decision
SADC	Southern African Development Community
tkm	ton-kilometer
TRAINS	Trade Analysis and Information System
TRC	Tanzania Railways Company
UNCTAD	United Nations Conference on Trade and Development
VAT	value added tax
VOC	vehicle operating cost
WAEMU	West African Economic and Monetary Union

All tons in this book are metric tons.

CHAPTER 1

Introduction and Overview

The objective of the study is to examine, identify, and quantify the factors behind Africa's high prices for road transport. Such prices are a major obstacle to economic growth in the region, as shown in several studies. For example, Amjadi and Yeats (1995) concluded that transport costs in Africa were a higher trade barrier than were import tariffs and trade restrictions. Other analyses by the World Bank (2007a) demonstrated that Africa's transport prices were high compared to the value of the goods transported and that transport predictability and reliability were low by international standards. This study's findings should help policy makers take actions that will reduce transport costs to domestic and international trade.

Past Research on Transport Prices and Costs

A few empirical studies, including trucking surveys carried out since the mid-1990s, demonstrated that transport prices were high in Africa compared with other regions. One study (Rizet and Hine 1993) estimated that road transport in three Francophone African countries (Cameroon, Côte d'Ivoire, and Mali) was up to six times more expensive than in Pakistan and about 40 percent more expensive than in France (where labor rates are much higher). Another study comparing seven countries in three continents demonstrated that for distances up to 300 kilometers, the unit costs of road transport in Africa were 40–100 percent more than rates in South east Asia (Rizet and Gwet 1998). Transport prices for most African landlocked countries range from 15 to 20 percent of import costs (MacKellar et al. 2002)—a figure three to four times more than in most developed countries.

Key factors that raise costs include low productivity of the trucking industry in Africa, notably because of infrastructure constraints (Pedersen 2001); low levels of competition between service providers (Rizet and Hine 1993); and weak infrastructure (Limao and Venables 2001). Limao and Venables also suggested that weak infrastructure accounted for most of Africa's poor trade performance. From a cross-country regression, they concluded that trade was highly sensitive to transport costs. For example, a 10 percent drop in transport costs increases trade by 25 percent.

In the past, it was presumed that large investments in improving road infrastructure would reduce transport prices. Since the 1970s, the World Bank has actively supported improvements to the transport corridors in Africa, including much support focused almost exclusively on improving infrastructure (see annex 1). Although such improvements facilitated road transport and reduced costs for the trucks carrying cargo on the corridors, no clear impact on the transport prices was evident. Furthermore, the end users of road transport services did not seem to fully benefit from the lower transport costs and better service quality resulting from improved infrastructure.

A review of the African corridor projects by the World Bank's Independent Evaluation Group (IEG)[1] found that most projects covered only a single transport mode or agency and focused on the development or rehabilitation of physical facilities. These Bank projects did not establish the prerequisites for future operations, such as regional agreements on corridor operations and streamlining and harmonization of regulation affecting transport. Neither the IEG review nor other studies attempted to explain why the reduction in operating costs did not result in lower transport prices.

Scope and Methodology of This Study

Scope. The study focuses on four key international corridors in Africa's subregions that connect ports of entry and exit to the hinterland (see map 1). In these corridors, the study analyzes transport costs and prices by grouping a number of factors into three main categories: (i) infrastructure, namely road network quality and coverage; (ii) factor costs, such as fuel, labor, and equipment; and (iii) market economics, including regulation, companies' organization, and transport and trade procedures.

The four corridors selected for the study[2] cover 13 countries in Africa's four subregions carrying more than 70 percent of the international trade of the seven landlocked countries in the study.[3] The 13 countries served are as follows:

- **West Africa:**   Ghana, Niger, Burkina Faso, Togo
- **Central Africa:**   Cameroon, Chad, the Central African Republic
- **East Africa:**   Kenya, Uganda, Rwanda
- **Southern Africa:**   South Africa, Zimbabwe, Zambia

The transport corridors are reviewed by the following characteristics:

- geography (entry ports and landlocked areas served)
- corridor institutional structure and the degree of competition between corridors and transport modes
- shipping connections
- regulatory regime and market structure

Methodology. Since much past research has been inconclusive, this study attempts to expand both the breadth and depth of the research and can claim to be original in several areas. Primarily, this is the first comprehensive and practical effort in the past 15 years to measure and quantify the high transport costs and prices in Africa using clear empirical evidence. This is also the first attempt of its kind in Africa and worldwide to disaggregate input factors into three tiers of costs and prices: (i) transport prices or tariffs incurred by end users, (ii) transport costs incurred by commercial transport providers, and (iii) vehicle operating costs (VOCs). Logistics costs are not formally assessed here but only used to complement the analysis, as there is no agreed definition of logistics costs. However, in the context of this study, the term *logistics* may be defined as the process of planning, implementing, and controlling the efficient, cost-effective flow and storage of raw materials, in-process inventory, finished goods, and related information from point of origin to point of consumption. In other words, logistics costs encompass a much wider range of activities than do transport costs and include transaction costs (related to transport and trade processing of permits, customs, and standards), financial costs (such as inventory, storage, and security), and nonfinancial costs (such as insurance). Finally, this is the first study that clearly recognizes the regional diversity of Africa's transportation market and attempts to measure with the same yardstick the costs, prices, and performance of the transportation industry across the four subregions.

The study was carried out in three phases. Phase I comprised a large trucking survey aimed at understanding the operations of truck services. The survey was carried out in 7 countries, but with traffic implication of 13 countries under the four subregional corridors and conducted interviews of approximately 20 trucking companies and 60 owner-operators (see annex 3). Phase II comprised field visits to validate the preliminary findings derived from the trucking survey. Because the survey responses could not provide a full picture of country-specific constraints on road transport services, field visits were carried out[4] to supplement preliminary findings and collect qualitative information. This phase also attempted to identify policies that could help lower the cost and price of transport services. Phase III comprised quantitative analysis of the trucking survey, combined with the qualitative information from the field visits. A stakeholder's feedback workshop was organized to discuss the results of the study and the design of various policy recommendations in each of the four subregions.

Much can be done to help Africa reduce the burden of high transport prices. However, a clear diagnostic framework is missing, without which it is not possible to formulate appropriate policies and actions. This study aims to provide the needed diagnostic framework.

For the discrepancy between costs and prices to be analyzed, the distinction between the three tiers of cost factors needs to be clarified. This distinction is useful because transport prices may or may not reflect transport costs, and major parts of transport costs are basically based on VOCs. Also, VOCs are a good reflection of the quality of road infrastructure and the types of vehicles on the roads. A definition of the three tiers of cost factors is given in figure 1.1.

Analysis of the Transport Environment

With its low wage levels, Africa's transport costs and prices should be much lower—probably the lowest in the world—since the trucking industry is a labor-intensive activity. Paradoxically, Africa's high transport prices (especially in Central Africa) are accompanied by poor service quality, on average below other regions in the world. This is mainly a result of high profit markups. On the other hand, transport costs (costs to transport service providers) are not excessively high in Africa, compared with developed and most developing countries.

Figure 1.1   Various Definitions Related to Transport

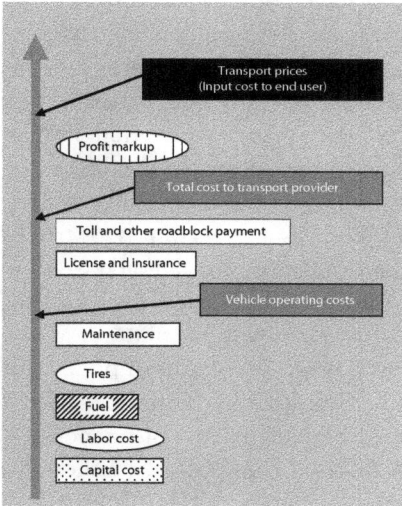

1. Transport prices are the rates charged by a transport company or a freight forwarder to the shipper or importer. Normally transport prices = TC's + operator's overhead and profit margin.

2. Transport costs (TC's) = VOCs + other indirect costs, such as license, insurance, road toll, and roadblocks payment.

3. Vehicle operating costs (VOCs) include various direct costs to operate a given vehicle, notably maintenance, tires, fuel, labor, and capital costs.

Source: Study team.

Logistics, regulation, competition. Among the logistics costs faced by the trucking industry are market entry barriers such as access restrictions, technical regulations, customs regulations, and cartels.[5] In Africa, the overall political economy of freight logistics exacerbates problems in trade and transport facilitation that are found worldwide. Logistics are fertile ground for rent-seeking activities such as corruption, protectionism, and inefficient trucking services, which in turn become a barrier to entry of modern operators. All these factors increase fragmentation and inhibit the emergence of the seamless supply chains needed by importers and exporters. Countries become trapped in vicious circles where inefficient regimes sustain low-quality services (including transport and customs broking) and high transport prices.

Of the market entry barriers, freight-sharing schemes probably are most costly. The current system favors the use of large fleets, which consist mostly of old trucks in poor condition. Furthermore, it fosters corruption because the only way for a transport provider to increase its volume of cargo is to bribe the freight bureaus, the government entities charged with allocating freight among the various transport providers. Freight-sharing schemes also are the reason why direct contracting—a negotiated arrangement between shipper and transporter that is one of the best signs of better logistics—is almost nonexistent in Central Africa and is marginal in West Africa. The freight allocation system is entrenched in these subregions, and several attempts to abolish it have not been successful.

In West and Central Africa, large markups by providers in transport cartels[6] are the main determinant of high transport prices. Cartels create a large gap between costs and prices and provide low quality. Operators in such markets achieve high profits despite low yearly utilization of their vehicle fleets and many nontariff barriers. Under such conditions, it would be expected that new operators would enter the market aggressively, but this does not happen. In fact, there is an oversupply of trucking capacity because outsiders find it hard to break into a market dominated by cartels and market access rules. In East Africa the trucking environment is more competitive and the market more mature. Major corridors in Southern Africa are the most advanced in terms of prices and efficiency of services, mainly because of a deregulated transport market.

Financing costs and import duties. Although the cost of financing is generally an issue for most sectors in Sub-Saharan Africa, neither the cost of financing trucks nor the level of custom duties (10 percent import tariff for large, new trucks) explains why truckers operate old fleets. Rather, old fleets persist in Central and West Africa because the regulatory systems in practice set a cap on truckers' revenues, deterring investment in new, high-cost trucks.

Truck overloading. In some subregions, excess transport capacity resulting from the freight allocation and queuing systems results in low levels of truck utilization and high transport prices. The two main strategies that operators undertake to mitigate low truck utilization are using secondhand trucks and overloading the trucks. Overloading is known to be a critical factor in damage to road structure and is therefore an important issue in many countries worldwide. Interventions in Africa by the World Bank and other donors to control overloading generally have not been successful. The reason, as determined by this study, is that most stakeholders in the trucking business have a vested interest in operating with overloads.

The impact of road conditions. In Sub-Saharan Africa, poor roads are perceived as being the main cause of high variable operating costs, since they increase fuel consumption, increase maintenance costs by damaging the vehicles, reduce the life of tires, reduce vehicle utilization because of lower speeds, and reduce the life of trucks. Results from the study suggest that poor road conditions along the selected Sub-Saharan Africa corridors do not add much to operating costs of trucks. The surveys and data simulations using the Highway Development and Maintenance Model 4

(HDM-4) the standard model for analyzing road investments, indicate a mixed result. In Central and West Africa, where traffic is low and the truck fleets are old, as long as international corridor routes are paved and in reasonable condition, further improvement of road conditions do not result in significant reduction of transport costs. However, in some East African corridors with higher traffic levels and newer fleets, improving road condition or increasing road capacity has a greater impact on reducing transport costs.

Different types of transport companies coexist on the same corridors. However, in general, the cost structure in Sub-Saharan Africa, even in the more modern and better-organized companies is, in general, different from developed countries: in Africa, trucking companies' variable costs are high while fixed costs are often low. Central and West Africa are the extreme cases with the variable costs to fixed costs ratios of 70/30, while in East Africa the ratio is 60/40. In contrast, in a developed system such as France, the variable to fixed costs ratio is 45/55. In all African corridors, fuel and lubricants are the main variable costs, accounting for at least 40 percent of total VOCS. Tires are another important cost factor, whereas bribes do not seem to play a major role as has been generally perceived on most African corridors.

Policy Recommendations

Policy recommendations need to distinguish between regulated and more mature market environments. In a competitive environment with high traffic volumes, measures to improve road conditions and limit fuel prices are likely to yield significant results. Furthermore, in such environments, measures aimed at reducing delays at the border or at weighbridges would also be useful as they would help increase truck utilization.

In regulated environments such as West and Central Africa, regulatory constraints (formal and informal) must be dismantled because they are the root cause of limited competition, poor service, and high transport prices. International experience has shown that deregulating the trucking industry is effective in generating more competition, lowering transport prices, and improving the quality of service in most cases (see table 2.1 in chapter 2).

West and Central Africa. In these subregions, the most effective measures to reduce transport costs are likely to be a decrease of fuel costs, an improvement of road condition, and, to a lesser extent, a reduction of border-crossing delays. Despite the perceived effects of informal payments,

Table 1.1   Measures and Outcomes in West and Central Africa

Measures	Decrease in transport costs (%)	Increase in sales (%)	Decrease in transport price (%)
Rehabilitation of corridor from fair to good	−5	NS	+/− 0
20% reduction of border crossing time	−1	+2 to +3	+/− 0
20% reduction of fuel price	−9	NS	+/− 0
20% reduction of informal payment	−1	NS	+/− 0

Source: Study team estimation based on trucking survey data.
NS = Not significant.

reducing them by 20 percent would have a marginal impact on transport costs. The analysis shows that improving road conditions from fair to good and reducing fuel prices by 20 percent could lead to reductions in transport costs by 5 percent and 9 percent, respectively (table 1.1).

However, such substantial reductions in transport costs would not lead to any reduction in transport prices because of the strongly regulated transport market in these regions. Therefore, any intervention should aim first at reforming cartels.

Breaking the regulatory status quo in many countries is difficult because of a coalition of interest groups against change. The corridors under review often are the main, and sometimes the only, transport mode for international and domestic trade. Therefore, truckers have strong leverage with high-level authorities who can block trade. Furthermore, some of these authorities own or indirectly control trucks or trucking companies and therefore benefit from the status quo and current market-sharing schemes.

Deregulating the trucking industry in West and Central Africa is less a technical than a political and social issue. The main concern is that under a liberalized, competitive market, the demand could be served efficiently by a much smaller number of trucks. This would lead to a drop in trucking employment and profits, since some companies (or owner-operators) would disappear and other would shrink. Participants in the stakeholders' workshops in Ouagadougou and Bangui emphasized the importance of mitigating the social impact of a more efficient but smaller trucking industry. There is a chance that the coalition of interest groups opposing change in the transport market in most of West and Central African countries might accept reforms as long as compensation schemes are introduced with the purpose of paying, at least partly, the social costs of such reforms.

East and Southern Africa. In these subregions, thanks to the competitive markets, and in contrast to the results in West and Central Africa, measures that would reduce transport costs would also lower transport prices. In East Africa, the most effective measures would be improving the condition of the corridor road and lowering fuel prices. Reducing the time of crossing the border would also have a positive although less significant impact. Reducing informal payments would have a minimal impact on costs, and no impact on transport prices.

In Southern Africa, reduction in border crossing time has the biggest impact on prices. This is mainly because the current delays in this corridor (especially at Beit Bridge and Chirundu) are at least twice as long (four days compared to a maximum of two) as at the Malaba border post in East Africa, and because of the more modern, pricier trucks used in Southern Africa. Creation of a one-stop border post would be the ideal solution for this corridor. The second most effective measure is a reduction in fuel prices, which has an impact similar to that in the East Africa corridor. Improvement in road conditions has a lower impact in Southern Africa because the road is in fair or good condition along the whole corridor. As in East Africa, reducing informal payments would have no large effect on the price of trucking services (see tables 1.2 and 1.3).

The study, therefore, concludes that the northern corridor in East Africa would be the only one where improving the physical condition of road would both (i) be economically justified, because it would substantially lower transport costs, and (ii) result in a decrease in transport prices. This conclusion also applies to the north-south corridor in Southern Africa subregion, but to a lesser extent. On the contrary, in West and

Table 1.2   Measures and Outcomes in East Africa

Measures	Decrease in transport costs (%)	Increase in sales (%)	Decrease in transport price (%)
Rehabilitation of corridor from fair to good	−15	NS	−7/−10
20% reduction of border-crossing time	−1/−2	+2/+3	−2/−3
20% reduction of fuel price	−12	NS	−6/−8
20% reduction of informal payment	−0.3	NS	+/−0

Source: Study team estimation based on trucking survey data.
NS = Not significant.

Table 1.3   Measures and Outcomes in Southern Africa

Measures	Decrease in transport costs (%)	Increase in sales (%)	Decrease in transport price (%)
Rehabilitation of corridor from fair to good	−3/−5	NS	−2/−3
20% reduction of border-crossing time	−3/−4	+18	−10/−15
20% reduction of fuel price	−10	NS	−5/−7
20% reduction of informal payment	−1	NS	+/−0

Source: Study team estimation based on trucking survey data.
NS = Not significant.

Central Africa, traffic levels are low and rehabilitation and upgrading cannot yet be economically justified for many sections of road. This is because cartels have steered the economic benefits of investment to a limited number of interest groups.

From recommendations to action. The measures listed above were tested by simulation analysis, and their importance confirmed in stakeholders' workshops in all four subregions. Converting the recommended measures into actionable policies should be done in the context of individual corridor and country conditions. Furthermore, policies should be examined in detailed, customized studies; such examination is outside the scope of this study. The following fiscal and other incentives are illustrative of measures that could be considered:

- *Create a more balanced tax structure.* This would lower the price of fuel, shifting more of the tax burden to vehicle registration in those cases where fuel tax revenues largely exceed reasonable road user charges. Tax balance would be especially helpful in inland countries where high domestic fuel prices hinder trade and negatively affect the competitiveness of trucking industries.
- *Change truck import duties to encourage the import of newer trucks or penalize the import of older trucks.* This can be done either by adjusting the current setting of import duties, which is proportional to the price of trucks, to a lump sum import duty or by progressive increase of import duties with the age of truck imported. This would encourage the modernization of the trucking fleet (in a competitive environment).
- *Find ways to provide direct monetary compensation to those truckers* who would become redundant when a more efficient trucking market was established following deregulation.

Role for the World Bank and development partners. Given the findings presented in this report, development partners, including the World Bank, should be encouraged to revise their development strategies. Transport services have been neglected for years under the assumption that reductions in VOC would automatically translate into lower transport costs, then transport prices. However, rent-seeking behaviors and poor governance of the trucking industry are central to many of the issues of low-income African countries. The list below suggests areas in which the donor community could help governments improve the efficiency of the transport market and eventually reduce transport prices.

- *Support transport market deregulation.* Support from development partners in this area would make the biggest impact in reducing transport prices in many countries in Africa. Successful institutional change such as breaking trucking cartels requires patience, continued policy dialogue, and strong support from development partners. Some partners might be inclined to drop their support if changes do not happen rapidly, but they should be aware that such actions could negatively affect several corridor projects.
- *Support the collection of trucking industry data.* Reliable data on the trucking fleet and operations are essential for analysis and policy formulation. Trucking surveys should be carried out periodically, probably every three to five years, as cost permits.
- *Support a review of the effect of fiscal policies on transport services*, especially in those countries where lowering the tax on fuel could be a useful instrument to reduce trade costs and to improve the competitiveness of the local trucking industry.
- *Support the use of country-specific trucking data in the economic analysis and design of road maintenance strategies.* Such analysis is, in most countries, done with the HDM-4 model, although country-specific trucking data are sparse. As a result, generic data with many assumptions are used in such model simulations. Data from trucking surveys could greatly improve the quality of the analysis and lead to more realistic results. One example is the need to introduce in the models the actual purchase price of the trucks, which in West and Central Africa often are bought secondhand, instead of using the price of new trucks. Using actual data would lead to different results, in particular reducing the possibility of overinvestment due to overestimation of investment benefit. If the investment analysis were done properly with realistic data, higher traffic levels might be needed to justify road improvements in some cases.

Following this introductory chapter, the study is organized as follows: Chapter 2 compares trucking in Africa with other regions. Chapter 3 reviews typical characteristics of the four study corridors, including an analysis of each corridor's transport market structure. Chapter 4 assesses the main determinants of transport prices and profitability, and chapter 5 demonstrates the impact of cartels on transport prices and service quality. Chapter 6 disentangles the main determinants of transport costs, and chapter 7 assesses the impact of road conditions on transport costs. Chapter 8 discusses perceptions about the trucking market, and chapter 9 analyzes the main measures aimed at lowering transport prices. Chapter 10 reviews the implications of the study for economic and fiscal analysis and for monitoring of the trucking industry. Chapter 11 presents conclusions and recommendations for ways international development agencies can support policies and for measures that could reduce transport prices.

Notes

1. World Bank (1994). This report covered 42 completed projects in 13 countries, including 7 landlocked countries (Rwanda, Burundi, Malawi, Zambia, the Central African Republic, Burkina Faso, and Mali) and six littoral countries (Kenya, Tanzania, Cameroon, Benin, Côte d'Ivoire, and Senegal).

2. **West Africa:** Cotonou–Ouagadougou, Cotonou–Niamey, Tema–Ouagadougou, Lomé–Ougadougou, Lomé–Niamey; **Central Africa:** Douala–Bangui, Douala–N'Djaména; **East Africa:** Mombasa–Kampala–Kigali; **Southern Africa:** Durban–Lusaka–Ndola.

3. Burkina Faso, Niger, the Central African Republic, Chad, Uganda, Rwanda, and Zambia.

4. The following field visits were carried out in June 2007: Burkina Faso/Niger/Benin, Cameroon/Central African Republic, Zambia/South Africa, Kenya/Rwanda.

5. In Africa, because of the thinness of some markets, cartels form more easily than in Asia or Europe. However, market thinness does not necessarily induce the existence of cartels, as the case of Rwanda demonstrates.

6. Cartels are composed of independent organizations or companies formed to limit competition by controlling the production and distribution of a product or service. Cartels can set monopoly prices, which induce abnormal markup.

CHAPTER 2

Trucking in Africa Compared with Other Regions

The performance of transport corridors in other regions, especially those in developing countries, can provide useful clues to assess the operations and costs of road transport in Africa. To this end, this chapter provides a brief comparison of road freight operations and markets on transport corridors in Africa with those in other regions. Subsequent chapters of this report analyze in more detail the situation in Africa.

The situation in no country or region is fully comparable with that in Africa, yet in each region specific similarities or policy reforms in road freight have been carried out that are of interest to Africa. Central Asia's countries have long distances to the sea, and many are landlocked as in Africa. Latin America has also two landlocked countries (Bolivia and Paraguay), which need to cross long distances to reach an ocean port. This region also offers useful experiences on transport deregulation, as does Central and Eastern Europe. Indonesia's deregulated road freight market is also of interest, especially due to the large proportion of small trucking companies. The Southeastern European countries trade mostly with countries outside their region, which is similar to the situation in Africa. In Pakistan, utilizing mostly old vehicles, many bought secondhand as in Africa, truckers manage to achieve very low transport costs and offer their services at low prices. Furthermore, Pakistan's road infrastructure on the main corridors is comparable in quality to that of the main corridors in Africa.

Transport costs on the main international corridors are not outrageously higher in Africa than elsewhere. But the paradox lies in the fact that with low wage levels, transport costs and prices should be much lower and probably the lowest in the world, as the trucking industry is intensive in labor.

Moreover, the four African subregions (West, Central, East, and Southern) are on average below other regions in the world with respect to transport quality, West Africa being the worst and Southern Africa being the best within Africa.

Global Comparisons

Transport prices. As shown in figure 2.1, transport prices in Africa are, on average,[1] higher than in South Asia or Brazil. Prices (per ton-kilometer (tkm)) on the Central African Douala–N'Djaména route (linking Cameroon with Chad) are more than three times higher than in Brazil and more than five times higher than in Pakistan. Only the Durban–Lusaka corridor in Southern Africa approaches the price level of other regions of the world.

Figure 2.1   Average Transport Prices: A Global Comparison in 2007

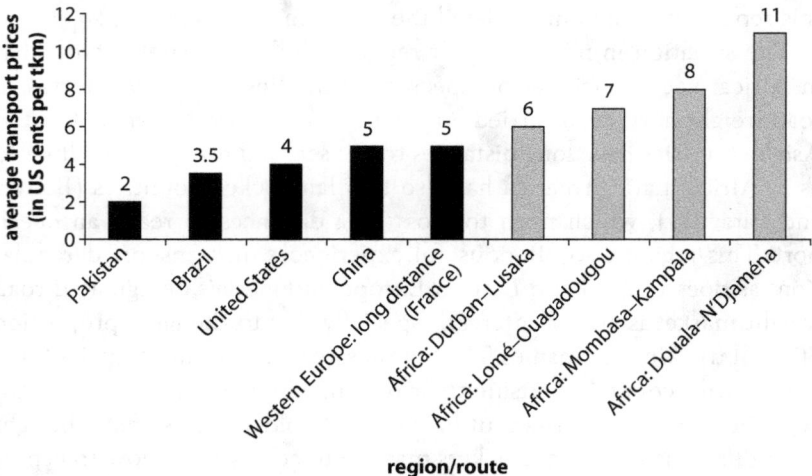

Source: Study team compilation of data from various sources.

Transport costs. Table 2.1 demonstrates that contrary to prices, transport costs on the main international corridors are not outrageously high. For instance, transport costs in Africa are not excessively higher than in Western Europe. Table 2.2 shows that indeed, variable costs in Africa are higher because of (i) high fuel costs; (ii) age of truck fleets, which leads to much higher fuel consumption; and (iii) road conditions that are probably the worst in the world. However, offsetting high variable costs, fixed costs are much lower in Africa than in Europe because of much lower wages and lower capital costs associated with aged trucks.

Despite such low wage levels, transport costs and prices were not much lower than in developed countries because of high variable costs. The trucking industry is labor intensive and, as such, the lower wages in Africa help to keep total transport costs down (see table 2.3).

Quality of service. A yearly survey of international freight forwarders allows the creation of a Logistics Performance Index (LPI).[2] The LPI, which is a useful indicator of quality of service, integrates a number of quality attributes into a single number. As shown in figure 2.2, the four African subregions considered in this study rank on average below other regions in the world on transport quality, West Africa being the worst and Southern Africa the best within Africa.

Transport price and quality. Comparing transport prices and the quality of service as measured by the LPI shows that Africa's transport is both more expensive and lower in quality than developed countries such as France and United States (figure 2.3). In the figure, the greater the LPI, the better the transport quality. The United States has an LPI of 3.84, whereas Africa ranges between 2.19 (West Africa) and 2.73 (Southern Africa). The Central African region is an extreme case of high prices associated with low quality.

The above findings are striking. Within individual markets it can be expected that higher-quality services command higher prices, since they normally cost more. Yet, as noted above, the comparison with other

Table 2.1   Comparative Transport Costs, Africa and Europe (Eastern and Western) in 2007

	Central Africa	East Africa	France	Spain	Germany	Poland
Transport costs per vehicle-kilometer (US$)	1.87	1.33	1.59	1.52	1.71	2.18

Source: Trucking Surveys for Africa, Comité National Routier (CNR) for Europe.

Table 2.2 Comparative Transport Costs, Central Africa, East Africa, and France in 2007

	Central Africa[a]	East Africa[b]	France
Variable costs (US$ per km)	1.31	0.98	0.72
Fixed costs (US$ per km)	0.57	0.35	0.87[c]
Total transport costs (US$ per km)	1.88	1.02	1.59
Average fleet age (years)	11	7	7
Fuel consumption (liters per 100 km)	65	60	34
Yearly mileage (km)	65,000	100,000[d]	121,000
Average daily speed (km per hour)[e]	30	43	69
Payload utilization[f] (percent)	75	76	87
Immobilization time before loading[g] (hours)	13	6	1.6
Articulated trucks (US$)	n.a.	169,200	138,000

Source: CNR for France. Trucking surveys for Central and East Africa.
Notes: East Africa truck price (in US$) corresponds to a heavy truck.
n.a. = Not applicable
a. Douala–N'Djaména corridor.
b. Mombasa–Kampala corridor.
c. Data for 2006.
d. Based on interviews.
e. Data from HDM-4 for African corridors.
f. Ratio of the number of kilometers with payload over the total number of kilometers of a truck. Data are based on rather similar truck capacity; African companies usually importing trucks from Europe after several years of use.
g. Calculations for immobilization time before loading for African routes come from the trucking surveys when loading at ports, in particular the following question: What was the average amount of time you waited to pick up freight once inside the port?

Table 2.3   Median Monthly Wages for Truckers in 2007

Country	Median monthly wages (US$)
France	3,129
Germany	3,937
Chad	189
Kenya	269
Zambia	160

Source: CNR for France and Germany. Trucking surveys for Chad and Kenya.
For France and Germany, monthly wages include bonuses.

Figure 2.2   Transport Quality Worldwide Based on the Logistics Performance Index in 2007

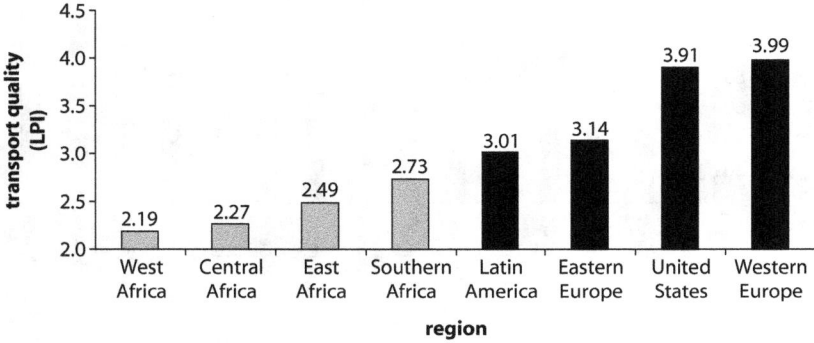

Source: World Bank, LPI (2007).

Figure 2.3   Transport Services in Africa—Expensive and Low Quality in 2007

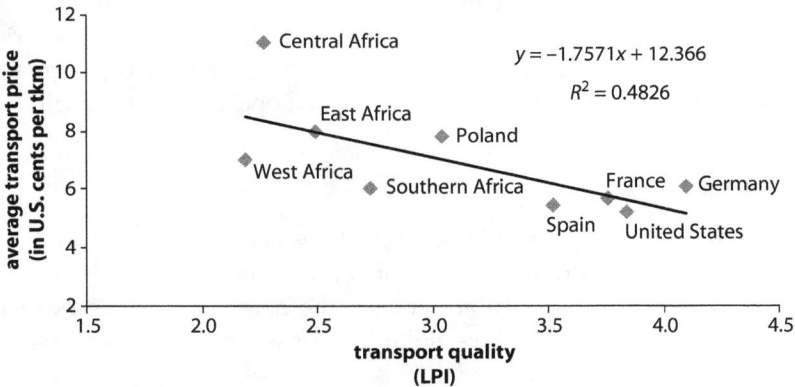

Source: World Bank and task team compilation from various sources.

countries shows that transport services in Africa are both pricier (in most cases) and significantly lower in quality.

Efficiency. Figure 2.4 compares truck utilization in Africa with that in selected developing countries. The figure shows, on the one hand, a large disparity among the African countries, with South Africa's trucks traveling almost three times as many miles as trucks in Malawi. On the other hand, trucks in other developing countries also show a large disparity in truck utilization, with Pakistan's trucks doing twice as many miles as China's trucks. It is striking that the trucks in the higher-income countries in Eastern

Figure 2.4   Average Truck Mileage in Selected Developing Countries in 2007

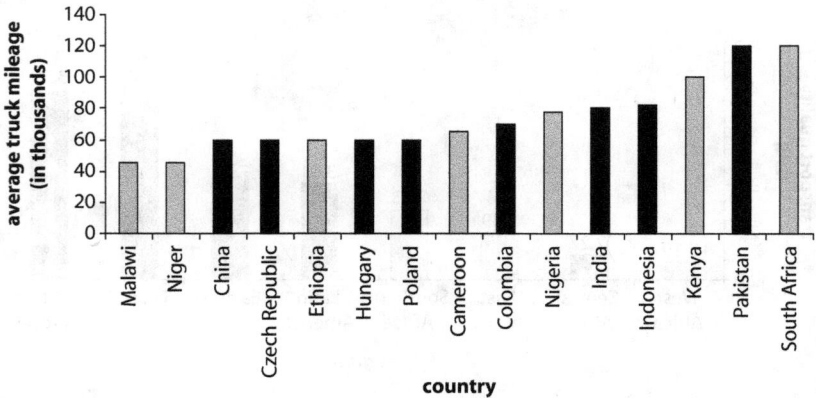

Source: Londoño-Kent (2007) and trucking surveys for African countries.

Europe are not utilized efficiently. This is mainly explained by the fact that there are relatively few trucking companies established in these countries that operate across borders. Thus, yearly mileage within countries remains lower than it would be if the companies would operate transnationally.[3]

Regional Perspectives

Trade. An important aspect of the operations and performance of international transport corridors is the nature of trade. In Africa, partly because of the similarity in production between the neighboring countries and partly because of infrastructure and other barriers to trade, most trade is international and not subregional. This means that trade logistics encompass not only land transport, but also ports and shipping issues.

On other continents, there are varying situations. In Latin America, an important part of exports in Bolivia and Paraguay go as final destination to neighboring countries, Argentina or Brazil. In Southeastern Europe, there was little trade among the countries. Sub-regional trade comprising only about 6 percent of total external trade in 2000.[4]

Operational issues. In the Southeastern European transport corridors, the key problems directly related to international road transport include some that are common to Sub-Saharan Africa, such as excessive waiting times at the border for clearing customs, and others that are more peculiar to the region. Such problems include difficulties in obtaining visas for professional drivers, lack of bilateral trip permits, and slow implementation of innovation in logistics.

Central Asian countries have the longest distances to an ocean port of any region in the world. The capitals of four Central Asian countries are 3,000 kilometers or more away from an ocean port. By comparison, distances to a port in Africa are mostly in the 1,000–1,500 kilometer range, with only three countries (Zambia, Rwanda, and the Central African Republic) being in the 1,500–2,000 kilometer range.[5]

In Latin America, the two landlocked countries, Bolivia and Paraguay, have some similarities with the international corridors in Africa in that they need to transit through other countries for export-import trade. The main international trade corridors run through Bolivia, which uses ports on both the Pacific and the Atlantic to connect with overseas markets. Paraguay's main route for both exports and imports is from Asunción to the duty-free port of Paranagua in Brazil. There is also important corridor traffic by road between maritime countries. For example, Brazil's trade crosses Argentina to reach Latin American countries on the Pacific or to use their ports for overseas trade with Asia. The cost of crossing international borders varies greatly in Latin America, with some of the higher-cost (both in monetary and time dimensions) border crossings occurring between maritime countries (for example, between Argentina and Brazil), rather than between Bolivia or Paraguay and their transit countries.

South Asia shares many similarities regarding trade and international transport with Sub-Saharan Africa: (i) both regions have a gross domestic product (GDP) per capita below US$1,000 (average US$684 for South Asia and US$830 for Sub-Saharan Africa); (ii) both regions trade less than 10 percent of the exports and imports within the region; and (iii) both have poor-quality transport facilities and services along international trade corridors. Yet there are important differences in how the corridors operate. In South Asia, a key factor explaining why transport corridors operate poorly is that national policies of most countries in the region prohibit access of foreign trucks. As a result, freight needs to be transshipped at the border from one country's trucks to the next country's trucks. Road transport costs in South Asia are the lowest in the world. However, the high cost of transshipment at the border, coupled with other problems in the logistics chain, negate the benefits of low trucking cost when international transport is concerned. Transshipment not only dramatically increases transport cost, but also poses a high risk to the condition of the cargo.

Pakistan's National Trade Corridor (NTC) provides an excellent example of the operations of a national corridor, with a mix of good and bad features.[6] The NTC links the Afghan border, close to Peshawar, through Lahore to Karachi and Port Qasim, with a link to Khunjrab. The NTC handles the major part of Pakistan's external and internal trade. In many respects, Pakistan's external transport and trade facilitation systems provide an adequate level of connection with the global economy. For instance, Pakistan's sea freight rates are in line with regional and international levels; its sea transit times are better for some major markets than for its competitors, and worse for others (largely a result of geography and distance); and its road transport rates are some of the lowest in the world. However, the system has a number of weaknesses that result in high cost and poor quality of service to the users. Major weaknesses include high port costs and rates; high dwell time for inbound containers; poor road transport services, with long transit times and unreliable service quality; the use of old and technologically outdated trucks, a result of import regulations and tariff structure; and poor road infrastructure with low capacity and quality not suitable for rapid and reliable truck services. Unfortunately, one of the main reasons for the low trucking costs in Pakistan is not efficient operation but a very high level of overloading, causing major damage to the roads. Some of these weaknesses can be removed by investments, but others require policy changes and freedom for the private sector to make its own decisions and investments.

Market Regulation, Competition, and Prices in the Trucking Industry

The prices charged for transport services and the quality of service depend substantially on the regulatory regimes and competitiveness in the trucking industry. International experience shows the benefits of strong competition in the trucking industry.

Many countries have over the past two decades introduced substantial reforms to their trucking markets, by essentially deregulating the industry. Selected examples are described below.[7]

Mexico. Until 1989, trucking in Mexico was strongly regulated, as in most of Latin America. Regulation was thought to promote fair pricing, prevent dangerous cost-cutting competition, and control quality of service. In practice, regulation served to restrict competition and limit supply to a few firms, resulting in high prices and poor service.

The government decided to deregulate trucking and did this gradually with changes effected over a two-year period (1989–90) with very positive impact.

Significant outcomes of the deregulation were as follows:

- Many new truck operators entered the market. Within a few months of completing the deregulation process in 1990, some 30,000 permits were issued for new entrants.
- Within five years, road transport prices had dropped by 23 percent in real terms.
- Trucking services improved in frequency, access, and speed of delivery.
- More flexible pricing of both truck and rail increased competition in the provision of transport services and helped to lower overall transport costs.

Today, after almost two decades of deregulation, the benefits remain, although some problems remain to be fixed, such as the need for states and local governments to complete harmonization agreements, the lack of which affects market structure and facilitates the rebuilding of cartels.

Indonesia. As part of a major liberalization of the transport market, road transport prices were freed in 1985. Since then, prices have been set by the market. Liberalization caused a large increase in the number of truck operators, creating a competitive market. The majority of public transport companies own only a small number of vehicles, although some operators own relatively large fleets. One of the restrictions to route freedom is that freight vehicles are required to obtain licenses to cross provincial boundaries, but such regulation does not seem to cause major economic distortions.

The Czech Republic, Hungary, and Poland. Road freight transport was one of the first sectors to be privatized and liberalized in most of the Central and East European countries. Hungary, followed by Poland and then the Czech Republic, was the earliest to adopt pro-competition reforms. Hungary and Poland passed laws granting free entry to the trucking market in 1988, as did the Czech Republic after 1990. Market forces freely determine transport prices. The combination of privatization and liberalization, which included deregulation reforms such as elimination of rate and route controls, led to the entry of many new trucking operators with competitive prices and better-quality services. A consequence of the new competitive environment included several innovative logistics services initiated by the trucking companies, resulting in faster delivery times and less breakage or spoilage of cargo. In most cases, the more significant service innovations were started by the larger, internationally connected trucking companies.

France. The 1986 deregulation of road transport in France led to dramatic lowering of road transport prices, as shown in figure 2.5. Comparing the relevant cost and price indexes, the figure clearly demonstrates a parallel trend of cost and price movement before the deregulation and a sharp divergence after the deregulation.

Morocco. Initial conditions of the transport services market matter for the success of transport liberalization. Morocco is a relevant example in this regard since liberalization induced strong price decreases but also diminished transport quality.

For decades, road freight transport was strongly regulated, with the monopoly of freight allocation carried out by the Office National du Transport (ONT). However, because of the ONT fleet's low productivity, many individuals invested in trucks and oversupply gradually increased.

Figure 2.5   Cost and Price Trends before and after Market Deregulation in France, 1980–97

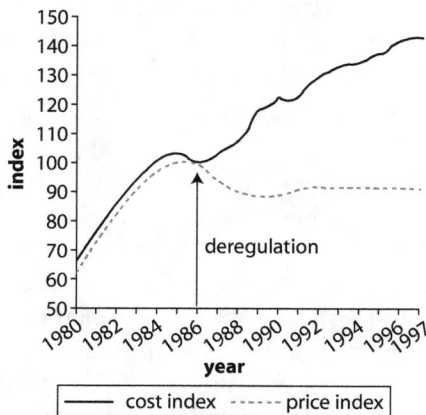

Source: Darbéra (1998).

In 2003, the Law 16-99 entered into force and abolished the monopoly of freight allocation for the ONT, and transport prices became deregulated.

Because of the initial large oversupply, along with exacerbated competition and low professionalism among individual operators, transport prices decreased for years and reached a level below transport costs, with a subsequent low quality of transport service. As a result, the Moroccan fleet has continued to age, drivers have remained untrained, and informal service predominates.

As a result, the Moroccan transport market is characterized by the following:

- a predominance of the informal sector, estimated at 70–75 percent of total freight transport in Morocco
- atomized supply with 90 percent of companies operating one or two trucks
- aging trucks (with 13 years as a median fleet age)
- average transport price below transport costs on most national corridors

An African experience: Rwanda. The only deregulation experience in the African region so far took place in Rwanda in 1994, and it had a huge effect on transport prices, confirming the impact that cartels have had elsewhere. After deregulation of international transport, prices declined by more than 30 percent in nominal terms and by almost 75 percent in real terms when taking into account the continued increase in input prices (figure 2.6). The impact in Rwanda was probably stronger than in most other countries because before deregulation road freight services were a monopoly of a parastatal trucking company (STIR) that was able to set high prices without any restraint (Mwase 2003). Furthermore, 1994 was also the bloodiest period of the Rwandan Civil War, when for all practical purposes a road freight fleet had ceased to exist.

Deregulation not only resulted in lower prices, but also led to growth in the Rwandan fleet. This is in contrast to common fears that deregulation, which liberalizes market entry, leads to eradication of the fleet owned by truckers from landlocked countries. In the case of Rwanda, the fear was even stronger given the disappearance of its trucking fleet at the height of the Civil War in 1994. In fact, deregulation helped to achieve a rapid recovery of the domestically owned fleet. A distinctive feature of the business strategy followed by Rwandan truckers has been

Figure 2.6   Average Transport Prices from Mombasa to Kigali
(US$, constant and current)

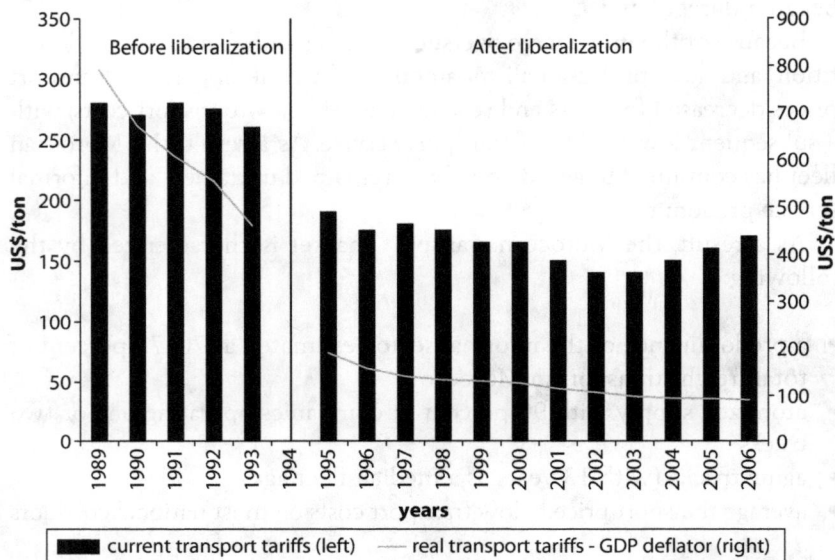

Source: Data from the Northern Corridor Transport and Transit Authority (NCTTA).

Figure 2.7   Number of Registered Heavy Trucks in Rwanda

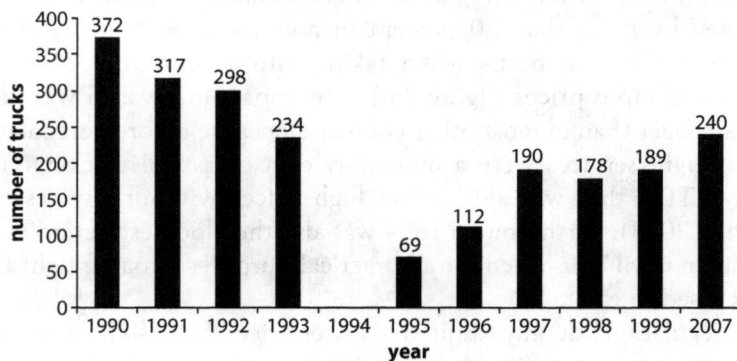

Source: Data from NCTTA.

their specialization in specific goods to capture niche and profitable markets, such as petroleum products. This largely explains why the current fleet is equal to the level prior to deregulation of international transport (see figure 2.7).

Malawi. This was a case of attempted protection of the local trucking industry against competition from truckers from other countries,
mainly South Africa. With that purpose, the Malawi government
established a surtax on domestic transport in Malawi. Under the current tax system, the domestic transporter collects the surtax on transport from the customer.

The surtax in fact served no purpose, other than hurting farmers who
had to pay the surtax for transport of their production, reducing their
profit margins, and providing the local truckers with additional profit for
their services. Market regulations in any case provided a strong entry barrier to South African truckers entering into the Malawi transport market,
where the government intended to protect the domestic road transport
providers. In the hypothetical case of real competition, the South African
operator would have remained much more competitive than the local
operator, as shown in table 2.4.

Thus, overall, trucking deregulation has been successful, leading to
more competition, lower prices, and better services, while attempts to
artificially protect local transporters (Malawi) have had perverse consequences. Table 2.5 summarizes the reform experiences.

Table 2.4   Comparison of Malawi and South African Fleet Competitiveness

Combination vehicle	Malawi New	Malawi Used	South Africa
Km/year	100,800	100,800	100,800
Load in tons	28	28	28
Payload utilization	75%	75%	75%
Ratios, cost per km	*US$*	*US$*	*US$*
Tires	0.110	0.110	0.060
Fuel and top-up oil	0.560	0.560	0.300
Maintenance	0.130	0.150	0.120
Overhead	0.100	0.040	0.100
Depreciation	0.230	0.060	0.120
Capital	0.540	0.100	0.060
Transit fees	0.170	0.170	0.125
Insurance	0.210	0.002	0.080
Licenses and permits	0.010	0.010	0.015
Driver wages	0.010	0.010	0.100
Total per km	2.064	1.21	1.080
Tkm	0.098	0.058	0.051

Source: Tera International (2005).

Table 2.5   Summary of World Experiences in Transport Services Deregulation

Country	Main achievements	Background
Czech Republic, Hungary, Poland	Entry of many new operators Prices determined by market Innovative logistics services	Major reform in 1998–90. Road freight transport was one of the first sectors to be privatized and liberalized in Central and Eastern European countries.
France	Dramatic reduction in transport prices	Major reform in 1986. Some 10 years after deregulation, overall prices increased by 40%, transport prices fell by over 10%.
Indonesia	Entry of many new operators Prices set by the market Most trucking companies small	Major reform in 1985. Vehicles were required to obtain licenses to cross provincial boundaries, but there was no major impact.
Mexico	Entry of many new operators Transport prices dropped by 23% in real terms within five years Trucking services improved in frequency, access, and speed of delivery	Major reform in 1989. The deregulation process was gradual over a period of two years.
Morocco	Transport prices dropped dramatically Abolition of government monopoly of freight allocation	Freight allocation abolished in 2003. Large initial oversupply was not reduced and led to atomized and low quality of service, but prices were reduced.
Rwanda	Transport prices fell by 75% in real terms Rapid recovery of locally owned fleet	Major reform in 1994. Reform occurred after the genocide, when the public trucking fleet had practically vanished.

Source: Task team compilation from various sources.

Notes

1. Average transport prices are difficult to disaggregate because transport prices or freight rates/tariffs are dependent on several factors including the following: (i) *return cargo*—if backload is ensured, freight rates are lowered; (ii) *cargo types*—tankers, oil products, machinery, and containers are more expensive to transport than general cargo in bags; (iii) *commercial practices/discounts*—there are often large discrepancies between published tariff schedules and what customers actually pay; (iv) *seasonal demand*—prices are seasonal and are highly sensitive to supply/demand, especially for certain export commodities and some imported finished goods.

However, although there are some possible biases and problems concerning data reliability, transport prices are rather homogeneous along the studied routes in the trucking surveys. Along a corridor, prices obviously vary: for instance, in U.S. dollars per ton-kilometer, from Mombasa, average prices are set at 4 cents per ton-kilometer for Kenya, 8.5 for Uganda, 9 for Rwanda, 11 for Burundi, and 12 for Democratic Republic of the Congo (from Goma) (Oyer 2007).

2. The LPI measures perceptions of the logistics environment of 140 countries on several dimensions (such as transport price, infrastructure, and customs). The survey uses an anonymous, Web-based questionnaire that asks respondents to evaluate their country of residence, as well as eight countries they are dealing with, on the following logistics dimensions: international transportation costs, domestic transportation costs, timeliness of shipments, tractability of shipments, transport and IT infrastructure, customs and other border procedures, and logistics competence.

3. CNR (2005).

4. World Bank (2004).

5. Kazakhstan, Kyrgyzstan, Tajikistan, and Uzbekistan. These figures are quoted in Snow et al. (2003).

6. World Bank (2007b).

7. Presentation of these examples draws substantially on three papers: Londoño-Kent (2007), World Bank (1994), and Dutz (2005).

CHAPTER 3

Key Logistics and Market Characteristics of the Transport Corridors

Logistics in Africa are organized along key trade and transport corridors originating from the ports of entry and exit to the hinterland.[1] In this chapter, the various transport corridors are characterized as follows:

- geography (entry ports and landlocked areas served)
- corridor institutional structure and the degree of competition between corridors and transport modes
- shipping connections
- regulatory regime and market structure

Table 3.1 shows the key international trade corridors from ports to their hinterlands. Table 3.2 shows the economic importance and volume of traffic for the relevant corridors.

The trucking environment and market structure in West and Central Africa are characterized by cartels offering low transport quality, while in East Africa the trucking environment is more competitive and more mature. Major corridors in Southern Africa are the most advanced of all the study corridors in terms of competitive and efficient services.

Table 3.1   The Four Key Transport Corridors in Africa: Ports and Countries

	Corridors			
	West Africa	*Central Africa*	*East Africa*	*Southern Africa*
Main ports of entry	Abidjan, Tema, Lomé, Cotonou, Dakar	Douala	Mombasa, Dar-es-Salaam	Durban, Maputo, Beira, Dar-es-Salaam
Landlocked countries served	Mali, Burkina, Niger	Chad, Central African Republic	Uganda, Rwanda, Burundi, Democratic Republic of Congo (east)	Botswana, Malawi, Zambia, Zimbabwe, Democratic Republic of Congo (south)

Source: Task team compilation.

Table 3.2   The Four Key Transport Corridors in Africa: Key Economic Data

Region and country	GDP (US$ billion)	Population (million)	GDP per capita (US$)	Annual imports (US$ million)	Annual exports (US$ million)
West Africa					
Togo	2.2	6.1	359	1,026	743
Benin	4.3	8.4	508	1,120	577
Ghana	10.7	22.1	485	6,610	3,869
Niger	3.4	14.0	244	825	512
Burkina Faso	5.2	13.2	391	1,132	449
Central Africa					
Cameroon	16.9	16.3	1,034	4,282	3,922
Central African Republic	1.4	4.0	339	174	126
Chad	5.5	9.8	561	2,150	3,219
East Africa					
Kenya	18.7	34.3	547	6,540	5,126
Rwanda	2.2	9.0	238	667	228
Uganda	8.7	28.8	303	2,370	1,145
Southern Africa					
South Africa	239.5	46.9	5,109	68,412	64,904
Zimbabwe	3.4	13.0	259	1,785	1,443
Zambia	7.3	11.7	623	1,835	1,192

Source: World Development Indicators, World Bank.
Date of all countries except the Central African Republic corresponds to year 2005, and Central African Republic to 2002. Amounts are in current market prices, U.S. dollars.

West Africa

Economic importance. West Africa comprises several gateways (Ghana, Benin, Côte d'Ivoire, Senegal, Guinea, and Togo) and three inland countries (Burkina Faso, Mali, and Niger). The 2002 crisis in Côte d'Ivoire, which resulted in the closing of the international road and rail routes starting from Abidjan, caused a rerouting of freight to other ports in Togo, Benin, and Ghana. For Burkina Faso, the rerouting resulted in Lomé and Tema increasing their share of the country's trade (for Lomé, from 20 percent in 1999 to 50 percent in 2004, and for Tema, from 7 percent to 36 percent during the same period). The crisis also affected Mali traffic, and as a result Burkina Faso became a transit country for Mali trade.

Trucking environment and market structure. West Africa is characterized by strong market regulation through freight bureaus and shippers' councils (see chapter 5 and annex 4 for more details). The quality of transport services is uniformly low. There are no large trucking

Figure 3.1   A Typology of Transport Corridors in Africa Based on Market Access

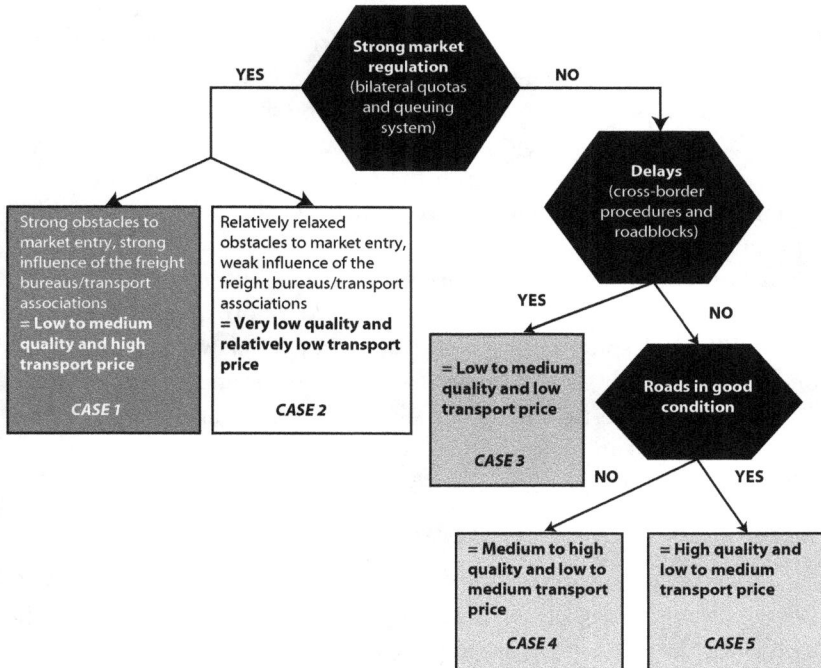

Source: Task team.
Note: Figure 3.1 defines a typology of corridors with market access at the core of the distinction.

companies and few new trucks, yet transport prices are relatively low (case 2 in figure 3.1).[2]

Central Africa

Economic importance. Traditionally, the regional transport industry in Central Africa, particularly with respect to transit traffic, has been shared between the road and road-rail corridors originating from the gateway port of Douala and the rail-river-road corridors between Pointe-Noire (the Republic of Congo) or Matadi (the Democratic Republic of Congo [DRC]) and Bangui in the Central African Republic (rail-river) up to N'Djaména in Chad. However, the rail-river corridor has lost all its market shares of the Chadian trade since the early 1990s and has become marginal for the Central African Republic trade (except for oil products through Matadi).

The regional transport industry thus is mainly dominated today by two road and road-rail corridors that link the port of Douala to the capital cities of the Central African Republic and Chad. These corridors provide the economic lifeline between the coastal (Cameroon) and the two landlocked countries (Chad and the Central African Republic). Besides the two capital cities, two other subregions play a crucial role for international trade. These are the southwest region in Chad, where most of the country's cotton exports and all the country's oil exports are produced, and the southwest forest region in the Central African Republic, where the logging industry is concentrated. Thus, Douala is one of the most important ports in West and Central Africa.

Trucking environment and market structure. Central Africa's international transport is characterized by cartels. Transport quality is low but prices are high despite the fact that prices may differ widely along corridors of the region. In this subregion, freight bureaus and transport associations are very powerful and do not allow many truck operators to bypass the system (case 1 in figure 3.1).

The Northern Corridor in East Africa

Economic importance. The long-established northern corridor runs from the port of Mombasa via Nairobi to Kampala, with extensions to the Democratic Republic of Congo, Rwanda, and Burundi. Mombasa, the largest port in East Africa, is well endowed with equipment and facilities, has a natural port whose berths do not require constant dredging, and has an adequate dock infrastructure. Mombasa now handles more than 13 million tons a year. Although intraregional trade in the East African Community (EAC) has been growing fast in recent years, it contributes only 20 percent of the trade volume in the subregion, while more than 80 percent of the trade flows are still going to and coming from outside the region. This corridor is now taking a new political and economic dimension with the recently reformed EAC, the regional organization of Kenya, Uganda, and Tanzania.

Trucking environment and market structure. East Africa is a competitive and mature market with "rates determined by market forces," especially for corridors originating from the port (Oyer 2007) (cases 3 and 4 in figure 3.1).[3] The largest professionalized trucking companies account for approximately 20 percent of total market shares according to our estimates,[4] which is comparable to any mature trucking market in Europe or North America. There are about 20 large companies that operate more than 100 trucks each. The largest Kenyan company owns a fleet of 600 trucks. These large companies obtain loads from long-term direct contracting (from one to three years). Their yearly mileage to Kampala can reach more than 100,000 kilometers, which is much higher than the average mileage in Central Africa (at most 60,000 kilometers per year).

Transport quality in East Africa is higher than in Central or West Africa, with larger and more modern truck fleets. However, on average, transport prices are lower, especially services to Uganda. There is no abnormal disconnect between prices and costs along the Northern Corridor (up to Kampala).

The North-South Corridor in Southern Africa

Economic importance. Four main trade corridors link Zambia and the southeast Democratic Republic of Congo to the subregion and overseas markets. These are Dar-es-Salaam, Walvis Bay, Beira, and the north-south corridor through Durban. The north-south corridor serves a dual purpose: First, it serves as an intraregional trade route between Zambia (and further southeast, the Democratic Republic of Congo and western Malawi) and its neighbors, Botswana, Zimbabwe, and South Africa, and as a link to the port of Durban for overseas imports and exports. From south to north, the two main border crossing points are Beit Bridge between South Africa and Zimbabwe, and Groblers Bridge/Martins Drift between South Africa and Botswana. Beit Bridge is the busiest border post in the region, handling as many as 500 trucks per day, whereas volumes through Martins Drift are about half that number.

Freight demand in Zambia has been rising rapidly with the opening of new mines, the increase of copper prices, and the growth of the economy (see annex 5). In 2005, approximately 1.6 million tons were exported, and 3.3 million tons were imported. The main exports from Zambia are mineral and agricultural commodities. The main imports, volumewise, were mineral products, chemicals, heavy mining equipment, and manufactured goods. However, valuewise, Zambia's main imports were machinery and mechanical appliances, fuels, electrical machinery, and vehicles.

Although the port of Beira in Mozambique is closer than Durban for most Zambian shippers, Durban is more convenient as it can be accessed directly by reliable road infrastructure and with channel-dredging equipment. Durban's port equipment and lower maritime transport rates make it also attractive for Zambian shippers.[5]

Durban is the largest port in the area, accounting for at least three-quarters of the total capacity provided by the various ports serving the corridors in the subregion. The Durban–Lusaka corridor route is then the most utilized corridor for Zambia.

Trucking environment and market structure. The Southern Africa corridor is the most advanced of all corridors in this study, both in terms of regulatory regimes and efficiency of logistics services[6] (cases 4 and 5 in figure 3.1).

The transport market and operations in Southern Africa are of great interest for other countries in the subregion because they combine liberalization with enforcement of quality and load control rules applicable to all trucking operators.

Operations to and from Southern Africa are governed by bilateral agreements. Unlike West and Central Africa, the Southern African agreements do not establish quotas. This enables direct contracting between shippers and transporters and creates incentives for transporters to be more efficient. The agreements contain the following provisions, among others:

- restrict the carriage of bilateral trade to carriers from the two countries
- prohibit cabotage
- provide that the regulatory authorities of the two parties shall share information concerning traffic development
- define the types of permits that may be issued, namely 14 days, short term (3 months), and long term (12 months)

- state that cargo rates and charges shall be determined by the market
- provide for the establishment of a joint route management group to determine transport needs on a route, among other things

Notes

1. Southern Africa is slightly different as a significant proportion of the import traffic into neighboring countries originates from the industrial core of South Africa and not from overseas through Durban.

2. Prices are relatively low compared with international standards, but this does not prevent profitability.

3. As in Central Africa, prices and profits may widely differ. Some oligopolies may be found on some marginal international routes, for instance after Kampala.

4. This is confirmed by Oyer (2007) who surveyed 15 percent of Kenyan trucking companies.

5. Since Durban is the hub port of the subregions, operators often prefer to truck containers directly from this port over longer distances instead of adding a feeder link to less well served but closer ports.

6. For the Durban–Johannesburg corridor, the rail market remains relatively important with 20 percent of the total market share (CSIR 2006, 18).

CHAPTER 4

Main Determinants of Transport Prices and Trucking Profitability

This chapter presents the findings obtained from the data gathered in the trucking survey relating to prices and profitability. The main findings from the study indicated that transport prices in Sub-Saharan Africa differ widely depending mainly on market regulation and structure. In a strongly regulated and noncompetitive environment, prices and profits are especially high, trucking along many international corridors being a strong seller's market and a profitable industry for most companies in Africa.

Heterogeneity of Transport Prices in Africa

Transport prices differ widely in Africa. In Southern Africa they are, on average, two to three times lower than in Central Africa. Some subregions such as Central Africa are characterized by a large spread in transport prices, explained by the fact that some large trucking companies subcontract to truckers at a much lower price, and others operate in a complete informal market with low prices and extremely low transport quality.

Transport prices and time. These vary greatly between subregions. Central Africa is the most expensive, West and East Africa have similar prices, and Southern Africa is the cheapest. Transport time is also a good indicator of quality of service. There are discrepancies in transport times

from cargo arrival at the port to the hinterland destination; the highest
delivery speeds are in West and Southern Africa whereas the lowest
reported speed is in Central Africa (see table 4.1).

Price factors. Data from the trucking survey provide clues about the
importance of cartels as a preeminent price factor in Africa, but there are
other important factors in international transport. The findings also signal
that transport practices, prices, and costs mainly are route specific.

The Importance of Rail Competition for Road Freight Prices

On the main international corridors, an absence of rail services creates
opportunities for the trucking industry to inflate its prices. That is why
intermodal competition on these corridors is critical. Increased competition from rail services benefits transport users primarily through comparable or lower transport costs.[1] Actual or potential competition from
road operators drastically limits the railways' pricing power,[2] even in the
situations where railways enjoy commanding market shares (World
Bank 2006).

Figure 4.1 compares rail and road prices in East and Central Africa. In
East Africa, road prices are established by trucking companies and take

Table 4.1   Transit Time and Transport Price (from Gateway to Destination)

Gateway	Destination	Distance (km)	Transit time from ship arrival to final destination	Transport price (in US$ per ton)
West Africa				
Lomé	Ouagadougou	1,050	6–8 days	60–70
Cotonou	Niamey	1,000	6–8 days	65–95
Central Africa				
Douala	N'Djaména	1,830	12–15 days	200–210
Douala	Bangui	1,450	8–10 days	200–210
East Africa				
Mombasa	Kampala	1,145	5–6 days	90
Mombasa	Kigali	1,700	8–10 days	100–110
Southern Africa				
Durban	Lusaka	2,300	8–9 days	90–130
Durban	Ndola	2,700	9–10 days	130–170

Source: Surveys of trucking companies and international logistics operators.
Note: Because of traffic imbalance, export prices are at most equal to import prices. However, in most cases,
export prices are lower than import prices because to avoid coming back empty, truckers prefer to give
discounts to get backload.

Figure 4.1   Road-Rail Price Competition in Main International Routes
(US$ per ton-kilometer)

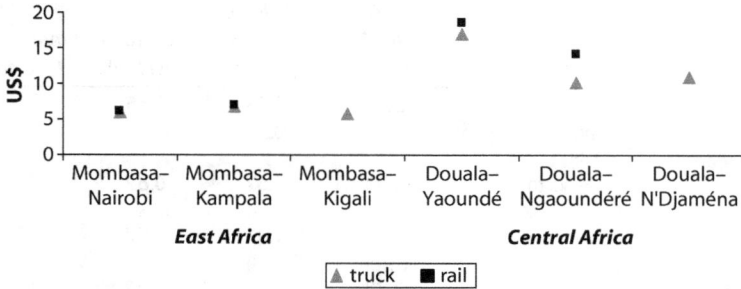

Source: Trucking survey and own calculations. Prices are per container.

into account rail prices. Therefore, competition between rail and road transportation does exist.[3]

Similarly, in Central Africa, rail prices are comparable to road prices. As in East Africa, trucking companies surveyed acknowledged that rail competition plays a role in the setting prices, especially for heavy and bulk commodities.[4]

Profitability Determinants

Trucking is a profitable industry for most companies in Africa, especially along the main international corridors (see table 4.2). Managers of trucking companies acknowledge, for example, that paying back costs of a new or less than three-year-old truck takes less than three years. In the many African countries where transport demand, as a result of economic growth, is booming, truckers can rapidly recover costs. Road transport has turned to a strong sellers' market almost everywhere in Africa.

Profits are a function of market size and the number of market participants. In Africa, because of the thinness of some markets, the cartels are easier to form than in Asia or Europe. However, this does not necessarily induce the existence of cartels, as we demonstrated in the case of Rwanda.

Fixed costs are abnormally high for Africa along the Douala–Bangui and the Ngaoundéré–Moundou corridors due to the extremely low yearly vehicle mileage (used as a proxy to measure efficiency of trucking service provision)—not because truckers use new trucks.

Standard deviation measures are especially high for prices. As noted above, this can be explained by the strategy of some large trucking

Table 4.2   International Transport Prices, Costs, and Profit Margins (from Gateway to Destination)

	Route gateway–destination[a]	Price[f] (US$ per km)	Variable cost (US$ per km)	Fixed cost (US$ per km)	Profit margin[i,h,c] (percent)
West Africa (Burkina and Ghana)	Tema/Accra–Ouagadougou (Ghana)	**3.53**[g] (2.01)	**1.54** (0.59)	**0.66** (0.64)	80
	Tema/Accra–Bamako (Mali)	**3.93** (1.53)	**1.67** (0.23)	**0.62** (0.36)	80
Central Africa (Cameroon and Chad)	Douala–N'Djaména (Chad)	**3.19** (1.10)	**1.31** (0.32)	**0.57** (0.30)	73
	Douala–Bangui (Central African Republic)	**3.78** (1.30)	**1.21** (0.35)	**1.08** (0.81)	83
	Ngaoundéré–N'Djaména (Chad)	**5.37** (1.44)	**1.83** (0.25)	**0.73** (0.44)	118
	Ngaoundéré–Moundou (Chad)	**9.71** (2.58)	**2.49** (0.64)	**1.55** (0.43)	163
East Africa (Kenya and Uganda)	Mombasa–Kampala[b] (Uganda)	**2.22** (1.08)	**0.98**[h] (0.47)	**0.35** (0.14)	86
	Mombasa–Nairobi[c] (Kenya)	**2.26** (1.36)	**0.83** (0.17)	**0.53** (0.19)	66
Southern Africa (Zambia)	Lusaka–Johannesburg[d] (South Africa)	**2.32** (1.59)	**1.54** (0.41)	**0.34** (0.40)	18
	Lusaka–Dar-es-Salaam[e] (Tanzania)	**2.55** (0.08)	**1.34** (0.52)	**0.44** (0.51)	62

Source: Trucking survey data and own calculations. Exchange rates come from International Monetary Fund-International Financial Statistics.

Note: Prices are in US$ per kilometer because most companies have the same truck capacity and similar (over)loading practices on a corridor. Moreover, because of questions in reporting overloading, prices in US$ per kilometer are probably much more reliable than prices per ton-kilometer. Prices and costs were obtained from reported truckload (approximately 30 metric tons). Values include trucking services (three or more trucks) and truckers (one or two trucks). Standard deviation is in parentheses.

a. Destination country is in parentheses.

b. First segment of the northern corridor

c. Second segment of the northern corridor

d. First segment of the north-south corridor

e. Second segment of the north-south corridor

f. Some indicative prices are set by ministries of transportation in Africa but are not used. Prices set by freight allocation bureaus in Central Africa may be more respected.

g. Prices from the trucking survey are similar to the ones given by the Conseil Burkinabe des Chargeurs (see table below). Depending on the tonnage (official or real), prices per ton-kilometers may be more or less higher.

h. Data should be taken cautiously since some companies may omit some costs or, conversely, double count some costs.

Unit	Official data from Burkina Faso shippers' council		Survey
	FCFA	US$	US$
Ton	26,000–30,000	52–60	59
Container	1,300,000–1,400,000	2,600–2,800	2,000

Note: Exchange rate US$/FCFA = 0.002.

i. Data are consistent with Oyer (2007), who found US$1.10 per kilometer for Kenyan routes, without including overheads and management costs or border-crossing and bribes costs.

companies, especially in a regulated environment, to subcontract freight to truckers at lower prices.[5] Consequently, some small subcontractors and truckers charge a low price and can hardly be profitable whereas some well-known trucking companies benefit from the regulated price and consequently reap large profits. Subcontracting also explains why old and new trucks travel along the same corridor. In most cases, new fleets indicate abnormally high markups, whereas old trucks belong to the subcontractors of a well-known trucking company.

Even though prices are relatively low in West Africa on the main international corridors compared with those in Central Africa, this does not prevent the trucking business from being profitable. Truckers keep production costs low through the combination of low capital costs (purchase of secondhand trucks) and minimal maintenance expenditures while maximizing revenues through overloading.

Success can rapidly turn into failure in the African transport industry and vice versa. If all the right conditions are attained (a "good" manager who gets access to the load, "good" drivers who find loads by themselves while limiting negative impacts to the truck, and a "good" truck that is reliable and cheap to maintain), then profitability can be high as the return on investment may average three years. Truckers who are unable to attain such conditions will not be profitable.

The various pricing strategies are all the more interesting, standard deviation being much lower for variable transport costs. In other words, most companies bear more or less similar variable costs, which by far are the most important determinants of transport costs.

Transport prices determinants. Table 4.3 confirms most of the findings from descriptive statistics. However, there is a very strong disconnect between costs and prices, especially for Central Africa, where neither variable nor fixed costs explain the high transport prices in the subregion. In fact, for Central Africa, the usual prices determinants are not statistically significant if we accept (i) that overloading induces higher transport prices and (ii) that there is a tariff premium for international corridors compared with national corridors. More surprisingly, higher transport prices are reported for roads in better condition. For example, roads along the Ngaoundéré–Moundou corridor are in very good condition and have high prices. This is most likely due to informal market-sharing agreements (see the section on market regulation).

Similarly, in West Africa, it is difficult to explain how transport prices are not closely correlated with transport costs, which are closely related to road conditions and variable costs. High fixed costs may explain high transport prices, which probably are related to the fact that some operators

Table 4.3   Regressions to Identify the Main Determinants of Transport Prices

	West Africa	Central Africa	East Africa
Dependent variable: transport prices			
Variable costs	0.73	−0.09	0.11
	(0.84)	(0.37)	(0.58)
Fixed costs	**1.25****	0.15	**3.38****
	(0.63)	(0.15)	(1.38)
Yearly mileage	34.85	−3.01	4.24
	(20.14)	(7.15)	(4.80)
Average load	**0.08****	**0.12****	**0.05****
	(0.03)	(0.01)	(0.02)
Road condition	−3.87	**10.16****	**−31.64****
	(5.83)	(1.08)	(6.91)
Fleet size	**0.10****	−0.01	−0.01
	(0.02)	(0.01)	(0.00)
National	**3.68****	**−1.23****	**−3.56****
	(1.60)	(0.40)	(0.74)
Constant	−1.95	**−4.89****	**26.35****
	(5.11)	(0.91)	(5.95)
R^2	0.57	0.78	0.55
Observations	73	120	56
Routes	4	6	3

Source: Task team estimation based on the trucking survey data.
Note: ** implies significance at the 5 percent level and * at the 10 percent level. Standard deviation is shown in parentheses.

work with foreign companies that have special niches of the market enabling them to charge higher prices. This hypothesis is corroborated by the fact that larger fleet sizes charge higher prices. Foreign or large shippers require a large fleet to gain access to local companies. Furthermore, as in Central Africa, overloading induces higher transport prices. However, contrary to Central Africa, international corridors seem to be cheaper than national corridors. This is probably related to the fact that in the trucking survey samples, national corridors are mainly operated by the Ghanaian fleet, which is in better condition than the Burkina Faso fleet that operates internationally. In any case, cheaper international corridors demonstrate that transport prices are probably much more reasonable in West Africa than in Central Africa.

The northern corridor in East Africa presents a different story, one of the main determinants of transport prices being road condition. To corroborate donors' investment policies along the northern corridor, we can demonstrate that on roads in poor condition, transport companies charge much higher prices. As in West Africa, the extent of fixed costs explains transport prices, which demonstrates that many operators have a good sense of their fixed costs (contrary to the situation in Central Africa). Similar to the other subregions, overloading induces higher transport prices. Finally, like in West Africa, international corridors seem to be cheaper than national corridors, which means that companies operating in the subregion charge a premium price. The main reasons for this premium are explained in the following sections. In any event, international transport in the northern corridor seems to be much more costly than national Kenyan transport.

Profitability determinants. Trucking along international corridors is usually a profitable industry for most companies in Africa. There is a strong disconnect between costs and prices, but profits are relatively well explained by costs level (see table 4.4). Consequently, since price settings are more or less exogenous, the most profitable companies in Africa are the ones able to operate on routes with abnormal prices or with a certain degree of cost efficiency. That is why, in East Africa, trucks operating on roads in good condition are profitable (probably because of the fact that

Table 4.4   Regressions to Identify the Main Determinants of Margins

	West Africa	Central Africa	East Africa
Dependent variable: margins			
Variable costs	−0.59	**−0.78****	**−1.00****
	(0.41)	(0.20)	(0.39)
Fixed costs	−0.28	**−0.36****	1.75*
	(0.31)	(0.08)	(0.93)
Yearly mileage	**20.63****	0.59	4.56
	(9.77)	(3.81)	(3.24)
Average load	**0.03****	**0.06****	**0.04****
	(0.02)	(0.01)	(0.01)
Road condition	−2.41	**3.38****	**−21.24****
	(2.83)	(0.58)	(4.66)
Fleet size	**3.3E–02****	−3.3E–03	−4.6E–03*
	(1.1E–02)	(3.0E–03)	(2.8E–03)
National	**1.84****	−0.28	**−2.44****
	0.78	0.21	0.50
Constant	0.74	**−1.30****	**17.81****
	(2.48)	(0.48)	(4.02)
R^2	0.29	0.50	0.42
Observations	73	120	56
Routes	4	6	3

Source: Task team estimation based on the trucking survey data.
Note: ** implies significance at the 5 percent level and * at the 10 percent level. Standard deviation is shown in parentheses.

on roads in good condition, operators charge similar rates). Profitability is even more pronounced for international corridors. In Central Africa, higher fixed and variable costs result in lower margins. For all the subregions, overloading creates higher profits, which explains why this practice is so widespread. In Central Africa, as for prices, higher profits are reported for roads in better condition. Once again, this is probably because of informal market-sharing agreements. Finally, companies operating on national corridors in West Africa are more profitable than subregional corridors, which reiterates the fact that transport prices may not be so high for Burkina Faso companies when their costs are taken into account.

In a competitive environment like the international corridors in Southern Africa, margins are set at 10–15 percent, which means that any savings in transport costs can have a positive impact on trucking profitability and transport prices.

Prices are inflated through the whole logistics chain. In a regulated environment, even though profits from freight forwarders may be lower, transport remains largely profitable. Any overhead or abnormal payment is automatically included in the price for the end user. Integrated services—which include shipping lines activities, port operations, logistics platforms operations, freight forwarding, and sometimes rail concessions—usually give a better quality of service but considerably inflate prices on several segments of transport, such as port operations or logistics platforms. These integrated global operators frequently prevent other operators from increasing their market share and use their market power to keep prices at high levels.

Notes

1. One fundamental aspect of road-rail competition that affects tariff differences between these two modes relates to government's existing policies toward road users. Although it is not the intent of this work to address legislation, we note that long-standing policies to provide road infrastructure to users at less than full recovery costs create serious competition imbalances in the transport sector. Road infrastructure is usually financed through the government's general budget, implying significant cross-subsidies from nonroad to road users, leaving only a fraction of total costs to be financed by road users. This may not have mattered in the past as railways were owned and operated by governments (that is, total subsidies for road and rail were roughly the same). However, the introduction of private operators, which are expected to fully cover their infrastructure maintenance and rehabilitation

costs through users' fees, should alter significantly governments' thinking in this area.

2. The impact of road-rail competition appears, nevertheless, to differ noticeably from one corridor to another as the spread between average road and rail prices varied in 2003 from 44 percent (Sitarail) to 213 percent (TRC) (World Bank 2006).

3. The governments of Kenya and Uganda concluded and support a joint rail concession between Mombasa and Kampala.

4. There is a strong correlation between average freight hauling distance and rail market share: the longer the route, the stronger a rail operator's market share (World Bank 2006).

5. This dualism is common to many industries and is based on a product differentiation strategy. Probably standard deviation is high because both trucking companies and truckers were interviewed and have different pricing strategies.

CHAPTER 5

The Impact of Cartels on Transport Prices and Quality

The trucking survey indicates that a large markup or profit margin by transport providers, made possible by the current regulatory regime, is probably the main determinant of high transport prices along some international corridors, such as that in Central Africa. The large disconnect between the transport cost incurred by the service providers and the cost to the users (transport prices) signals the existence of a distorted transport market with a cartel.[1] Profits achieved despite low yearly utilization of the transporters' vehicle fleet and many nontariff barriers suggest that new operators would aggressively enter the market. Yet, this does not necessarily happen; the total fleet size does not increase. Furthermore, oversupply remains rampant. This is explained by the fact that operators already participate in the current system of market regulation (formal and informal) and outsiders may find it hard to operate in a market where compliance with operational regulation and market access rules is necessary.

The trucking industry in Sub-Saharan Africa faces various regulatory constraints, such as market entry barriers, market access restrictions, technical regulations, and customs regulations (table 5.1). However, market access restrictions through freight-sharing schemes have the largest impact on the performance of the trucking industry. The current system gives power to large fleets in poor condition and fosters corruption—the

Table 5.1 Main Regulatory Barriers in Sub-Saharan Africa

	West Africa	Central Africa	East Africa	Southern Africa
		Market entry		
Licenses	Not restrictive (especially for nationals)	Not restrictive (especially for nationals)	Not restrictive (especially for nationals)	Not restrictive
		Market access		
Bilateral agreement	Yes	Yes	No	Yes
Quotas/freight allocation	Yes	Yes	No	No
Queuing system	Yes	Yes	No	No
Third-country rule [a]	Prohibited	Prohibited	Prohibited	Allowed in some countries [b]
Technical regulation (road-user charges, axle load, vehicle standard, import restriction)	Problem of harmonization of axle-load regulation	Problem of harmonization of axle load enforcement	Problem of harmonization of axle load regulation, delays at weighbridges	Prohibition of secondhand imports in South Africa
Customs regulation	Cumbersome transit procedures inducing border-crossing delays	Cumbersome transit procedures inducing border-crossing delays	1. Prohibition for trailers in transit to pick up backloads in Kenya 2. Cumbersome transit procedures inducing border-crossing delays	Cumbersome transit procedures inducing border-crossing delays

Source: Study team compilation of data from various sources.

a. The third-country rule allows operation of trucks registered in a third-party country to transport goods between two other countries.

b. South Africa, Zimbabwe (on a reciprocal basis), and Malawi (during a defined period of time).

only way to increase transported volumes is to bribe the freight bureaus. This situation also explains why direct contracting, one of the best signs of better logistics, is almost nonexistent in Central Africa and marginal in West Africa. The freight allocation system is entrenched in these subregions and several attempts to abolish it have been unsuccessful.

The different levels of truck utilization in Sub-Saharan African subregions are the result of oversupply of transport capacity, which explains differences in transport prices. The two main strategies that operators use to mitigate regulatory burdens are the use of secondhand trucks and overloading. See box 5.1 for an illustration of how this system was abolished in the case of France.

Impact of Freight-Sharing Schemes

Market entry through the licensing process is relatively easy. Indeed, trucking companies and operators do not identify the licensing process as a main constraint of the sector. Moreover, except in Kenya and Uganda, licenses to operate internationally remain marginal expenses in total VOCs. Oversupply in many landlocked countries (see below) tends to demonstrate that market entry and credit access to finance trucks are not a major constraint to market entry.

However, customs regulations have a major impact on truck utilization and therefore on VOCs.[2] For instance, Kenya bans trucks used for international transit from transporting domestic goods on return trips, which leads to cutting in half the average payload utilization on the Mombasa–Kigali route. This is detrimental to trucking industry profitability. Moreover, cumbersome transit regimes induce delays at the borders, which can seriously limit truck utilization.[3]

Notably, the main regulatory issue concerns operational rules and market access restrictions, mainly through freight-sharing schemes. The regulatory environment of landlocked countries in West and Central Africa is centered on two related regulations:[4]

- a transit bilateral treaty, which establishes quotas for the fleets of the coastal and landlocked countries
- a formal/informal queuing system ("order of loading" or *tour de rôle*[5]) that allocates freight to transport companies, requiring the operator to be affiliated with a transporter association

Even though the *tour de rôle* is perceived negatively by most stakeholders in landlocked countries, the bilateral quotas are supported to protect truckers

Box 5.1

History and Impact of the Queuing System in France

The queuing system in France originated with inland water shipping. Established in 1936, the system was codified by the law of March 22, 1941. Queuing was applied to the road transport sector after the establishment of the regional freight bureaus (BRF) in 1961.

Freight bureaus receive transportation requests from shippers. After centralizing requests regionally, a list of vessels is assigned chronologically to the transport requests. The chronology of assignment mainly depends on when a carrier's availability registration arrives at the freight bureau.

The queuing system was set up by a decree of July 28, 1965, to "ensure the proper functioning of the freight transportation market and allow transport coordination." The BRF* took over coordinating supply and demand of transport, a task that cafés had once performed unofficially. Each carrier was registered on arrival at the BRF and then received a priority order to load freight.

Requests to the BRF for transportation always had to come from a transport broker. The request was displayed on a blackboard with key information (tonnage, destination, type of goods, and so forth). If a carrier was interested in fulfilling this request, an announcement was made in the office. If no other carrier claimed the same freight, the batch was assigned to the carrier that registered first. If the freight was claimed by another carrier, the first registered carrier got the load; however, two subsequent vehicles from the same carrier could not be loaded without a prescribed minimum delay. This system was established to prevent large companies from controlling the BRF.

What was the impact of such a system? The BRF increasingly became responsible for delays and poor transport quality. Indeed, guarantees of work made carriers complacent and competition nonexistent, which undermined transport service quality. Queuing did not lead to an optimal distribution of traffic or give incentives to provide better service, but led to an oversupply of trucks in a context of freight shortage. Oversupply could oblige a trucker to stop running a truck for a month or more. That also discouraged investment in new trucks, which created high risk for future revenues. The queuing system gave more power to large fleets in poor condition and fostered corruption, because the only way to increase transported volumes was to bribe the freight bureau.

In France, this system was abolished 20 years ago in the road transport sector and five years ago in the inland water shipping sector.

Source: Based on Souley (2001).
* France was divided into 19 regions. A national center, CNBRF, coordinated the work of the regional BRF.

from inland countries. In fact, in many countries in West and Central Africa, authorities have tried to tackle the problem by declaring the system (order of loading) unlawful. However, these attempts have not been very successful, mainly because the quota system gives a legal basis to restrictive practices.

A main justification for the queuing system is fairness and the possibility of sharing transport profits with small operators. The rationale is then social. Despite the fact that supporting services provided by national operators in developing countries may be laudable, in many cases the perceived benefits of market regulation in Sub-Saharan Africa are captured by a few people at the expense of the whole economy (see box 5.2 for the example of maritime transport).

Box 5.2

Captured Market Regulation: Cargo Reservation Schemes in Maritime Transport

The United Nations Convention on the Code of Conduct for Liner Conferences (UNCTAD 1975), which entered into force in 1983 with ratification by 78 countries, established the "40/40/20" Rule in maritime transport. The main provision of the rule was that shipments carried between two state parties had to be shared in the following way: 40 percent for shipowners established in the country of origin, 40 percent for shipowners established in the country of destination, and 20 percent for shipowners from other countries (cross-traders).

Justification of the rule
This cargo reservation scheme was promoted to encourage the development of the shipping industry in developing countries and to counteract the anticompetitive behaviors of the liner conferences,* which were cartel-like arrangements. The rule was meant to give developing countries the opportunity to participate in the carriage of their trade as a method to decrease the trade deficit in services as well as to induce international trade (Fink et al. 2002). With the acceptance of the Liner Code during the 1970s, the European conference members cooperated with the African maritime authorities to share traffic with new national African shipping companies.

Impact of the rule in developing countries
In general, the Liner Code has been counterproductive (Chasomeris 2005; European Commission 2005) because local shipping industries did not take off. As a result of the Code's distorting practices, maritime transport prices increased. The

(continued)

Box 5.2 *(Continued)*

"40/40/20" Rule led to a protected market for African shipping companies, an oligopolistic rent for European shipping lines, and strengthened vested interests in the sector. In reality, the rule created several national shipping companies without ships, which sold their country's share of cargo to foreign shipping lines without accepting any responsibility for the quality or cost of the services provided (Harding et al. 2007). In addition, the Liner Code sometimes was used as a justification for discriminatory practices that created market distortions. In some instances, the Code provisions were misused to justify the extension of the "40/40/20" Rule to the whole of liner trade or even to bulk transport.

The end of the rule

During the 1980s, it became increasingly difficult to keep some European and Asian members of the conferences out of the market, and in 1992 the European Court ruled that the liner conferences were illegal monopolies. In many West and Central Africa countries, the lifting of the "40/40/20" Rule has led to increased competition with Europe, which ultimately has led to decreased transport prices (Pedersen 2001). As a result of maritime transport liberalization (still only de facto in some countries) and the end of the rule, national shipping lines that had been established under the umbrella of the Liner Code greatly diminished in size and importance and were usually taken over by foreign shipping lines or went bankrupt.

Source: Task team based on Souley (2001).
* Shipping companies have organized themselves since the 19th century in the form of liner conferences, which fixed prices and regulated capacity. They are associations of shipowners operating on the same route served by a secretariat.

In road transport, bilateral transit treaties with quotas and freight allocation and the queuing system play the same role that the "40/40/20" Rule played in maritime transport. This system and rule lead to poor service and low productivity, with no incentives to improve efficiency.[6] So that transport quality could be assessed in such an environment, a measure of transport quality was developed that was based on trucking survey results.[7] The measure is a proxy for a transport quality index and is based on factors known to influence transport quality.[8] It includes the education level of the head of the company, the number of years in the industry for the head of the company, the perception of the importance of domestic competition, the importance of load obtained through contracting, the use of a tracking system, the fleet age and size, and the number of employees (see results in figure 5.1). According to this index, transport quality seems to be highest in Kenya and Uganda and lowest in Chad and Burkina Faso.

While bilateral freight allocation protects the trucking industry of landlocked countries, it creates de facto cartels and slows down market and regional integration. Furthermore, the protected operators often do not meet regulatory requirements. For instance, the Nigerien fleet is not appropriate to handle freight peaks and for various reasons is less competitive than are coastal countries' fleets.

In practice, authorities and trucking companies acknowledge that bilateral quotas are not enforced in the case of Niger.[9] Adoléhoumé (2007) estimated a 36 percent market share for the Nigerien fleet on the Togolese corridor in the first six months of 2007, whereas it should have been in theory two-thirds. The same figures are given for the Central African Republic and Cameroon. On the ground, landlocked countries' fleets do not carry more than 50 percent of total traffic because the fleets are inadequate and uncompetitive.

Adoléhoumé also estimated that the Nigerien fleet of articulated trucks is on average 29 years old, and its operating costs per vehicle-kilometer are some 30 percent higher than the Beninese or Togolese fleets. Shippers who are forced to use local fleets have to pay a surcharge that reflects higher prices, lower quality, or bribes (if shippers want to use their own transporters). These costs are detrimental to the interests of landlocked economies.

Figure 5.1   Transport Quality Index Based on the Trucking Survey Results

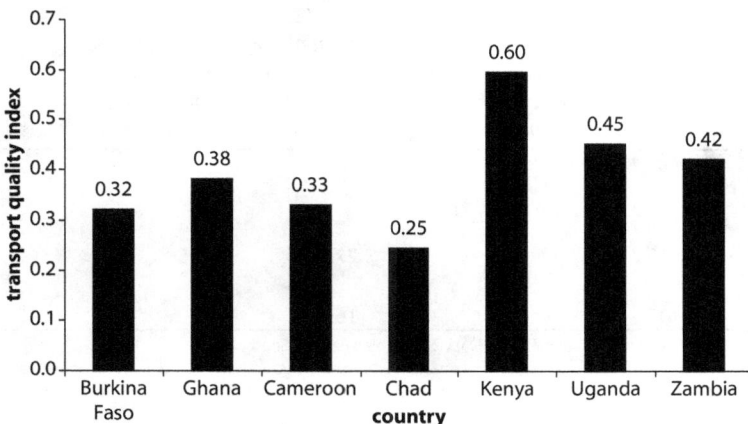

Source: Trucking survey and own calculations.

The bilateral quota system is prone to strengthen bribes because the trucking association in charge of enforcing quotas "sells" market shares and freight to truckers and trucking companies ready to pay the highest bribe. This helps explain why bilateral quotas are not enforced. Further, in the case of Niger, the trucking association frequently sells freight to non-Nigerien companies.[10]

Direct contracting—that is, a medium- or long-term contract between a shipper and a trucking company—is one of the best signs of good logistics. However, direct contracting is almost nonexistent in Central Africa and limited in West Africa to some institutional shippers, which bypass the queuing system (see table 5.2). Stakeholders and representatives of transport associations usually agree that such contracts are the only way to develop an efficient transport industry. That is why the importance of direct contracting is an excellent proxy to assess modernization, or the lack of, in the trucking industry.

Central and West Africa are clear examples of the negative effects of freight-sharing schemes on transport prices and quality. However, the freight allocation system entrenched in these subregions would not be easy to abolish. In Niger, there was a recent attempt to abolish the queuing system. A government decree[11] states that (i) the two-thirds and one-third rule to distribute traffic between local transport companies and the maritime transport companies is still in effect, but (ii) all trucking operations

Table 5.2   Main Methods Used by the Trucking Industry to Get Freight
(percentage by subregion)

	Through independent freight agents	Through public-private institutions in charge of freight allocations	By phone/fax and through contracts from customers	By trucks waiting at lorry parks and finding their own loads	Others
West Africa	42.7	21.0	**16.2**	1.9	18.2
Central Africa	35.7	11.4	**2.1**	24.1[a]	26.7
East Africa	12.7	20.7	**27.3**	5.1	34.2
Southern Africa	12.5	1.1	**16.4**	0.8	69.2

Source: Trucking survey and own calculations. Data for Zambian fleet for Southern Africa.
Note: It is difficult to capture the exact role of freight bureaus from the trucking survey. Interviews suggest that bureaus are more important than surveys because truckers with old fleets benefit from the current system.
a. This percentage, as well as the percentage of freight procured through independent agents, can be construed as part of the freight procured through allocation bureaus. Indeed, agents that "negotiate" with freight bureaus and truckers waiting at lorry parks depend on paperwork issued by the freight bureau.

within the Nigerien two-thirds are open to full competition.[12] Yet a workshop organized by the government on the Nigerien transport industry with all stakeholders to discuss the decree was boycotted by trucking associations.[13]

Up to now, the decree is nothing more than a signal. Indeed, the *tour de rôle* never had any legal ground and was designed by the Nigerien truckers to be self-imposed. Hence, its implementation requires willingness from Nigerien trucker association representatives. The queuing system will persist as long as transport associations have leverage, thanks to the bilateral transit agreement, which gives them the power to avoid direct contracting between the shipper and the transporter.

Occasionally, smart outsiders can enter this closed market, creating some competition. However, entering the market this way generally means long waiting times at the port and possible risks of retaliation from the trucking association or freight bureau.

Truck Age and Utilization

The large difference in transport prices (and costs) between Southern Africa on the one hand and Central and West Africa on the other is clearly correlated with the level of truck utilization and the oversupply level, which mainly depends on the existence of cartels. Although trucking companies in Southern Africa are able to utilize their vehicles at levels similar to European transporters (10,000–12,000 kilometers per month), operators in Central and West Africa utilize their vehicles at lower rates (sometimes as low as 2,000 kilometers per month).

The dismal truck utilization in West and Central Africa implies that the profitability of the trucking operations comes from other factors. One factor is the low capital investment where operators purchase old trucks. Table 5.3 shows that only 34 percent of truckers or trucking companies financed their vehicles, partially through a bank loan in Central Africa, and only 21 percent in West Africa. The cost of a truck, more so than financing costs, may explain why truckers buy low-cost and old vehicles. Figure 5.2 shows that fleet age is highest in West and Central Africa. These subregions also have the lowest yearly mileage because of cartels and oversupply.

Truck overloading. Another critical variable in the profitability of trucking is the load per truck. To maximize loads and revenues from limited trips and low vehicle utilization, operators need to overload their vehicles. Since the revenue of the transport providers is generated on a per-ton basis and the marginal cost of overload is low, overloading does make sense.[14]

Table 5.3   Method of Financing Truck Purchases
(percent)

	Financed by a bank	*Financed by company cash flow*	*Financed by personal savings*	*Financed informally*
West Africa	21	58	47	8
Central Africa	34	42	46	13
East Africa	53	53	54	5
Southern Africa	7	56	56	11

Source: Trucking survey and own calculations.
Note: Sum of columns exceeds 100 as often more than one method of financing is used for truck purchase.

Figure 5.2   Fleet Age and Yearly Mileage
(by subregion)

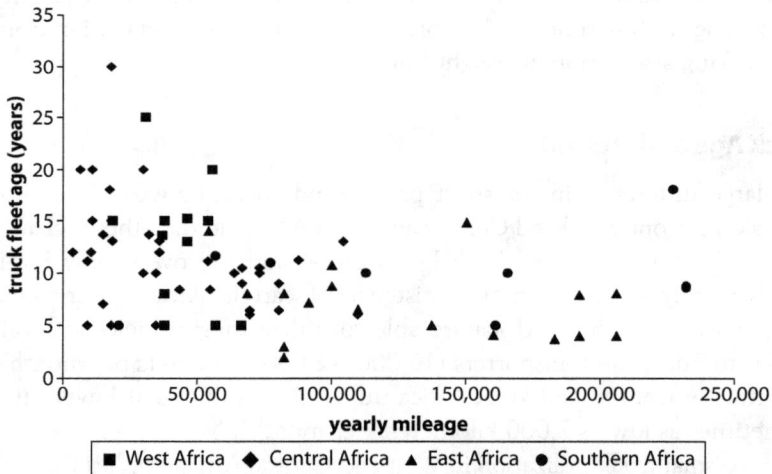

Source: Trucking survey and own calculations.

Most stakeholders in the trucking business have a vested interest in operating with overloads:[15]

• The driver is a direct beneficiary because he or she is paid cash for extra tons loaded but not declared. This may double or triple his or her salary (from FCFA 50,000 to FCFA 100,000 or even FCFA 150,000 per month).
• The head of the trucking company knows about this practice but disregards it as long as it does not have much impact on the truck.
• The intermediary also has a direct interest, his or her commission being calculated on the load for which he or she intermediates.

- The shipper also benefits since the load logged at the border will be the legal one, resulting in large savings on tariff duties.
- Law enforcement agents (including customs agents) who overlook the obvious overload are adequately rewarded.

The only loser of this systematic overload is the economy of the country, either directly through lower import tax revenues or indirectly through rapid road destruction.

Niger's public authorities, for example, have relaxed their policy regarding overloading penalties. According to regulations of the West African Economic and Monetary Union (WAEMU), a penalty of US$120 per overloading ton should be enforced on top of a flat penalty fee. However, in 2005, the government adopted a national regulation that reduced drastically the penalties for overloading. According to the old regulations, a truck with a 65-ton load (common in West Africa) should have been penalized more than US$1,000; the new regulation has reduced the overloading fee to US$25. This policy adjustment certainly benefits trucking companies and truckers, but it heavily taxes the general public, who have to pay for the premature deterioration of the country's road assets.

The use of weighbridges to control loads has been ineffective, and not just in Niger. As shown in table 5.4, several road sections with weighbridges are in no better condition than sections where there are fewer or no weighbridges. There is sufficient evidence to assume that overloading is the main cause of road deterioration and, therefore, that the weighbridges are not being utilized effectively to control overloading.

Table 5.4   Infrastructure Condition and Load Control

Region	Origin	Destination	Percentage of road section in good or fair condition	Number of weighbridges
West Africa	Tema/Accra	Ouagadougou	82	no data
	Tema/Accra	Bamako	61	no data
Central Africa	Douala	N'Djaména	45	7
	Douala	Bangui	53	6
	Ngaoundéré	Moundou	100	0
	Ngaoundéré	N'Djaména	61	2
East Africa	Mombasa	Kampala	86	4
	Kampala	Kigali	75	2
Southern Africa	Lusaka	Johannesburg	100	no data
	Lusaka	Dar-es-Salaam	no data	no data

Source: Task team calculations.
Note: Good or fair condition reflects the percentage of the section that could be traveled at 50 km/hour in all seasons.

A vicious circle of transport prices and costs. The combination of the regulation framework and the operators' mitigation strategies, including overloading, is illustrated in figure 5.3. Three main issues affect risk for truckers and shippers:

- limited market and oversupply, which makes freight scarce
- cumbersome public procedures (freight-sharing schemes, controls on goods in transit, border controls), which lead to truck underutilization
- high costs of inputs and technical risks (linked to old fleets operated on roads that may be in poor condition), which make truck utilization costly

Truckers' mitigation strategies are centered on the following issues:

- cartel formations
- overloading
- the use of secondhand vehicles

Cartels

Truckers have misconceptions about the benefits of cartels. One of cartels' negative consequences is oversupply. Indeed, this system attracts more truckers because of the *potential* profits and increases technical risks because of the fleet age and overloading practices. Freight bureaus are

Figure 5.3   The Vicious Circle of Transport Prices and Costs in a Strongly Regulated Environment

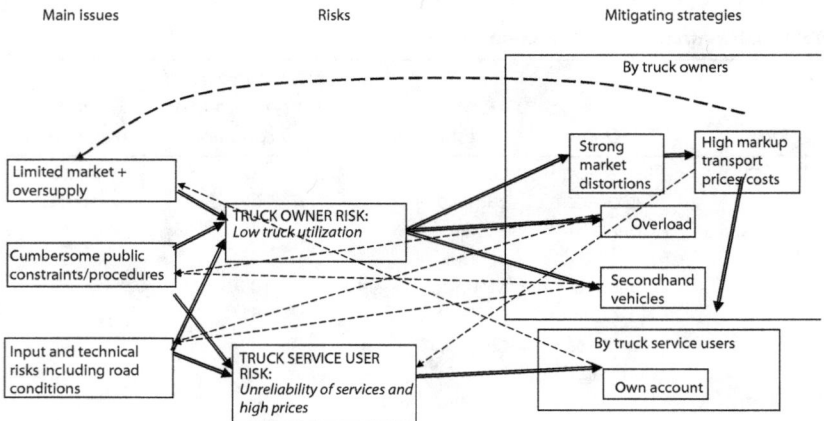

Source: Task team.

unconcerned, because as long as their fees (official and nonofficial) are paid, freight is allocated irrespective of whether oversupply is rampant. Consequently, there are too many trucks and not enough freight.

Moreover, many transporters may ultimately suffer instead of benefiting from the regulatory regime, since commercial trucking becomes less attractive to users. Indeed, shippers have to pay a high price for a low service quality—a strong incentive for widespread own-account transport. Representatives of transporters' associations usually single out own-account transport as one of the main reasons for market oversupply and unfair competition. However, they usually acknowledge that own-account transport is the result of the transport industry's poor performance.[16] For shippers, the main mitigation strategy is to develop own-account transport, which makes freight even more scarce for professional truckers. That is also why the model of trader-transporter is so widespread in West and Central Africa.

Fleet Size

What is the ideal fleet size for landlocked countries? Under the current traffic allocation assigning two-thirds of international freight to landlocked countries, their fleets are up to three times larger that needed for satisfactory levels of productivity for the capital invested in trucks.

Even considering long turnarounds and fleet characteristics, several landlocked countries have larger truck fleets than they need to meet current demand. This is partially explained by cartels. For example, the Central African Republic has a (theoretical) fleet of 600 trucks[17] for approximately 200,000 tons of exports and less than 100,000 tons of imports. Assuming about one-third of the fleet is composed of inactive or out-of-service trucks, this leaves about 395 trucks as the adjusted current active fleet. However, the demand—measured by current import/export volume—would only require 125 good-quality trucks to carry the current freight volume. In West Africa, the total Nigerien fleet is approximately 4,500 trucks. Applying the same one-third factor to discount trucks not in service, the operational fleet would still be three times larger than needed. With around 1 million tons of imports and two-thirds of the traffic for the Nigerien fleet, than 100 trucks per day are needed. Fewer with a turnaround of 15 days, its ideal size should be about 900 trucks (see table 5.5).

If freight quotas between coastal and landlocked countries' fleet were ended, the market share for Niger's and Burkina Faso's fleets would likely

Table 5.5 Current Trucking Demand and Ideal Supply, Central African Republic and Niger

Country	Adjusted current fleet[a]	Demand	Oversupply ratio	Ideal fleet	Oversupply/ideal fleet as percentage of current fleet
Central African Republic	395	125[b]	3.15	100[c]	6% (25 trucks)
Niger	2,970	905	3.30	455	15% (450 trucks)

Source: Adoléhoumé (2007) for Niger data and Ministry of Transport for the Central African Republic data.
a. Adjusted means total fleet less one-third.
b. 140,000 metric tons of exports are loaded in Belabo (return transport time from Central African Republic (CAR) to Belabo is at most 5 days); 90,000 metric tons of imports come from Douala (return transport time Douala to CAR is about 15 days). Without an overload of at least 10 percent (30 metric tons), we can estimate the average daily demand for 12 trucks to go to Belabo and 8 trucks from Douala. Because of long turnaround times, the total demand is (12 × 5) + (8 × 15), of which two-thirds is for the CAR fleet.
c. At the same current demand. Without overloading, we can estimate the average daily demand for 20 trucks to go to Belabo and 15 trucks from Douala. Because of shorter turnaround times, the total demand would be (19 × 3) + (12 × 8), of which two-thirds is for the CAR fleet.

decrease. Because of higher capacity resulting from increased truck productivity, the oversupply ratio in these countries would be higher than three, at least until their fleets gradually were downsized.

Notes

1. A cartel is a consortium of independent organizations or companies formed to limit competition and set monopoly prices by controlling the production and distribution of a product or service. Cartels induce abnormal markups.

2. An estimate of the impact of various measures is presented in chapter 10 of the report.

3. For more details on the impact of transit regimes on the trucking sector's competitiveness, see Arvis et al. (2007).

4. See annex 4 for more details.

5. Contrary to bilateral quotas, the *tour de rôle* has no legal basis whatsoever.

6. A landlocked country limiting access to its freight market for foreign companies self-imposes higher transport prices on its trade. Transport cannot be optimized with backloads, and transport providers, assuming no backload, charge higher prices one way.

7. It would have been better to assess transport quality from end users, but it is difficult to get reliable data on transport quality from surveys of firms, such as investment climate assessments.

8. The index is calculated as a weighted average of indexes using the following weights:

Parameter	Weighting coefficient
Education level of the head of the company	2
Experience in the industry of the head of the company	1
Perception of the importance of domestic competition	2
Importance of freight load obtained through contracting	2
Use of tracking system	1
Fleet size	1
Fleet age	3
Number of employees	1

9. This situation also was corroborated for Burkina Faso's trade flows during the stakeholders' workshop in Ouagadougou in February 2008.

10. International own-account transport is usually allocated to Beninese companies. Shippers willing to overload prefer to use Beninese or Togolese fleets, which are younger.

11. Ministerial decree number 09/MT/DTT-MF of February 2007.

12. The most important articles of the decree are the following:

"Article 2: Within the two-thirds quota allocated to trucks registered in Niger, the importer is authorized to load its cargo on its own truck or any Nigerien trucker's trucks of its choice with trucks registered in Niger (with valid transport and registration documents).

Article 4: The CNUT is in charge to monitor the repartition between Nigerien trucks and those from the transit country and will report it to the Minister of Transport.

All changes in truck assignments that violate the freight repartition as done by the *Comité Paritaire* will be fined according to the law."

13. Some companies attempt to enter the market without being part of a trucking association and of the queuing system, but usually on very limited niches.

14. The willingness for all parties to overload trucks to maximize profits does not favor containers, because their fixed maximum capacity prevents overloading. That is why containerization rates remain low in most parts of Africa.

15. Despite being unable to estimate overloading in detail, Oyer (2007) found a strong positive correlation between vehicle operating costs for heavy trucks and cargo factor.

16. This point was discussed at length during the stakeholders' workshop organized in Burkina Faso in February 2008.

17. Figure given by the CAR Ministry of Transport.

CHAPTER 6

Transport Costs Determinants

This chapter analyzes the factors influencing road transport costs. It starts by discussing the way companies organize and operate, and follows by suggesting a typology of companies, which is important since transport companies' organization affects both fixed and variable costs. It then presents a comparison of transport costs between the various corridors, and concludes with an analysis of variable and fixed costs as well as factors influencing them.

Based on the trucking survey carried out in this study, different typologies of transport companies coexist on the same corridors. In general, the cost structure in Sub-Saharan Africa is opposite from those in developed countries. In Africa, trucking companies' costs are mostly variable, while fixed costs are generally low. The extreme cases of high variable costs to fixed costs are in Central and West Africa (about a 70/30 ratio) whereas in East Africa the ratio is 60/40 between variable to fixed costs.

In all African corridors, the cost of fuel and lubricants are the main variable costs, accounting for at least 40 percent of total VOCs. Tire cost is also an important factor. On the other hand, bribes do not seem to play a major role on most African corridors.

In East and Southern Africa, transport costs are severely affected by the opportunity cost of delays (at border crossings, weighbridges, and ports) and long custom procedures.

Typology of Trucking Companies in Africa

The way companies organize themselves and operate influences their costs, both fixed and variable. Table 6.1 describes the typology of trucking companies, ranging from formal, professional companies to informal, owner-operator companies. Different types of trucking companies operate on the same corridor and face different costs, making it necessary to determine whether each type can compete and be profitable.

Operating Costs in the Subregions

Variable costs represent the bulk of total transport costs in Central and West Africa, with a minimum average ratio of 70/30 for variable/fixed costs; the main components of variable costs are fuel and tires.

Table 6.2 illustrates how the cost structure differs between African countries and developed countries. In developed countries the trucking industry is labor intensive, which explains why numerous companies in Western Europe employ cheap labor from Eastern Europe. In Africa, variable costs dominate, mainly fuel, tires, and, to a lesser extent, bribes in Central and West Africa. The cost of capital may also be a problem in East Africa.

Transport costs. Table 6.3 shows the average operating costs of selected routes in the four study corridors. The spread in transport costs is smaller than for transport prices. In general, variable operating costs[1] in African countries range between US$1.22 and US$1.83 per kilometer with the exception of high variable costs on the Ngaoundéré–Moundou route (US$2.49) and low variable costs on Mombasa–Kampala (US$0.98). On the other hand, fixed operating costs mainly depend on the routes. As shown in the table, daily fixed costs in Africa can vary threefold, from US$21 to US$73, but this variation is small compared to fixed costs observed in Europe or the United States.

Along Central African corridors,[2] routes that are comparable in distance and average fleet age (9–11 years) include Douala to N'Djaména (1,830 kilometers) and Douala to Bangui (1,450 kilometers). These routes have similar variable average operating costs, between US$1.22 and US$1.31 per kilometer. However, they do not have similar fixed operating costs since relatively newer fleets operate to Bangui compared with those operating to N'Djaména.

Comparable routes starting in Ngaoundéré (Cameroon) with final destination in Chad are Ngaoundéré–N'Djaména (750 kilometers) and Ngaoundéré–Moundou (460 kilometers). These routes have similar low fixed costs, around US$22 per day, but face different variable operating costs. This is mostly explained by the higher expenses in tires, maintenance

Table 6.1 A Typology of Trucking Companies in Africa

		Characteristics			
Type of company	Freight forwarding and transit activities	Own-account transport service	Fleet size	Fleet financing	Fleet operation characteristics	Comments
1. Modern—professional	Yes	No own-account transport	10 to 100+	Cash flow, leasing, and bank financing	High mileage (over 80,000 km/year) High fixed costs Usually own new trucks	High fixed costs; low to high transport prices depending on market regulation
2. Modern—informal	Yes	Own-account transport	10 to 100+	Mainly leasing second-hand vehicles with guarantees from traders	High mileage Lower fixed costs than professionals Lower total costs Mix of new and secondhand trucks	Cross-subsidy of activities and informality, which enables companies to offer lower transport prices and have large fleets
3. Formal—powerful	No	Usually no own-account transport	A few to dozens	Various financing but mainly cash flow	Low mileage (50,000–70,000 km/year) Low fixed costs except if prices are extremely high and allow for fleet improvement Mix of new and secondhand trucks	Companies' power (ties with political decision makers, position in trucking associations, law enforcement agents, including customs, police, and tax agents) allows them to circumvent rules. Huge profits in a regulated environment

(continued)

Table 6.1 A Typology of Trucking Companies in Africa (continued)

Type of company	Characteristics					
	Freight forwarding and transit activities	Own-account transport service	Fleet size	Fleet financing	Fleet operation characteristics	Comments
4. Own account	No	Own-account transport	Depends on the extent of industrial activities	Included in the funding of main activities	Low mileage New or secondhand truck; depends on the company strategy	
5. Informal—individuals	No	No own-account transport	Limited to 1–3 trucks	Cash flow	Low mileage (50,000–60,000 km/year) Low fixed costs Low revenues Secondhand trucks	Low transport prices because of oversupply of transport Low quality of service to remain competitive; informal costs (bribes) are a major cost factor

Source: Task team compilation.

Table 6.2   Transport Costs Composition
(percent)

Cost	France	Chad	Kenya
Fuel	25	50	21
Maintenance and tires	9	22	10
Depreciation and insurance	12	8	24
Toll roads/road-user charges	5	11	1
Staff costs	35	6	19
Administrative and overhead costs and others	14	3	25
Total	100	100	100

Source: CNR for France, trucking surveys for Chad and Kenya.

Table 6.3   Truck Operating Costs in the Four Corridors

Corridor	Route gateway/ destination	Variable cost (US$/km)	Fixed cost (US$/day)	Yearly ratio FC/VC (%)	Average truck fleet age (years)
West Africa (Burkina Faso and Ghana)	Tema/Accra– Ouagadougou (Burkina Faso)	1.51 *(0.59)*	30 *(16)*	10–89	13
	Tema/Accra–Bamako (Mali)	1.67 *(0.23)*	36 (23)	10–89	9
Central Africa (Cameroon and Chad)	Douala–N'Djaména (Chad)	1.31 *(0.34)*	49 *(30)*	17–82	11
	Douala–Bangui (the Central African Republic)	1.22 (0.34)	73 (43)	25–74	9
	Ngaoundéré– N'Djaména (Chad)	1.83 (0.27)	22 (8)	7–92	15
	Ngaoundéré– Moundou (Chad)	2.49 (0.64)	21 (6)	5–94	19
East Africa (Uganda and Kenya)	Mombasa–Kampala (Uganda)	0.98 (0.46)	61 (30)	68–31	7
	Kampala–Kigali (Rwanda)	1.47 (0.84)	40 (30)	56–43	10
Southern Africa (Zambia)	Lusaka–Johannesburg (South Africa)	1.54 (0.41)	55 (39)	61–38	9
	Lusaka–Dar-es-Salaam (Tanzania)	1.34 (0.52)	71 (54)	75–24	10

Source: Trucking survey data and own calculations. Exchange rates come from IMF-IFS.
Notes: FC = fixed costs; VC = variable costs; figures are averages with standard deviation shown in parentheses.

costs (old fleets operating to Moundou), and bribes.[3] On the Ngaoundéré–Moundou route, some trucks are almost 20 years old, despite the fact that a new, rehabilitated road is open to traffic (financed by the European Union).

In East Africa, a great discrepancy in the operating costs, both variable and fixed, exists on different corridors. A similar discrepancy exists within the same corridors between different trucking companies, mainly between those established in Uganda and Kenya. Kenyan companies face higher fixed costs than Ugandan companies. This is explained by Kenya's recent acquisition of a new fleet (incurring high depreciation and financial costs), low variable costs due to a more modern and efficient fleet, and good road conditions on the main corridors.

Operating costs in Southern Africa are similar to those in East Africa. Fixed costs and variable cost ratios are higher compared with those in the rest of Africa. The Zambian fleet, although older, manages to achieve higher yearly mileage than in East Africa, which creates certain cost disparities between these two subregions.

In West African countries, costs are relatively similar between national corridors. Variable operating costs in both cases are one standard deviation away from the average. Fixed operating costs are low, and the cost structure is similar to that of the Chadian companies.

Calculations in this study are based on trucking survey data and compute all costs,[4] which explains why our estimated fixed transport costs are much higher than transport costs estimated with models such as the HDM-4 (an extensively used methodology in many studies). It is worth noting that because the HDM-4 uses data for new trucks as an input, variable maintenance costs are higher than our estimates. However, fuel and lubricant costs are much higher in our estimates (using actual data of old trucks with less fuel efficiency) than the usual values calibrated using new trucks in the HDM-4. Overall, our estimated variable costs are higher than the ones developed by HDM-4. Table 6.4 compares the values obtained using the two different approaches.

Table 6.4   Comparison of Transport Costs for a Heavy Truck Using Alternative Methods of Analysis
(US$ per vehicle-km)

Costs	West Africa			Central Africa			East Africa			
	TS	HDM	Diff.	TS	HDM	Diff.	TS	HDM	Oyer	Diff.
Variable costs	1.77	1.02	**173%**	1.30	0.99	**131%**	0.98	1.08	0.95	**91%**
Fixed costs	1.02	0.14	**749%**	0.57	0.24	**236%**	0.35	0.17	0.15	**201%**
Total costs	2.79	1.16	**241%**	1.87	1.23	**152%**	1.33	1.25	1.10	**106%**

Source: Trucking survey data and own calculations.
Notes: TS = trucking survey; HDM = highway development maintenance model; Oyer (2007); Diff = difference.

The Importance of Variable Costs

Vehicle operating costs show a ratio of about 30/70 between fixed and variable costs in Central Africa, 40/60 in East Africa, and 15/85 in West Africa (table 6.3). Overall, operating costs for a heavy truck are as high (in Southern Africa) and sometimes much higher (in Central Africa) than in Europe.

Compared with European operators, African operators usually have lower fixed costs but higher variable costs. Low fixed costs (salary and equipment principally) can be attributed to the low cost of labor and the use of cheap, secondhand trucks (as old as 10–15 years). High variable costs can be attributed to high fuel consumption because of the trucks' characteristics—low capacity, old models, and poor maintenance. Because of the pervasive use of old trucks, average fuel consumption for trucks in Africa can be more than 50 liters per 100 kilometers, which is high by European standards.

In the corridors under review, the cost of fuel is the main variable cost. Three other variable costs—tires, maintenance, and bribes—are also important, although their contribution to variable costs depends on corridors (table 6.5).

In Central Africa, fuel and lubricants account for 38–60 percent of total variable costs. Bribes account for 27 percent of the total variable costs, which are sometimes equal to or higher than tire costs. The main fixed costs are staff (up to 38 percent) and depreciation. Financial costs

Table 6.5   Variable Costs Breakdown for Subregions
(percentage of total variable costs)

Corridor	Route gateway/ destination	Fuel	Tires	Maintenance	Bribes
West Africa	Tema/Accra– Ouagadougou	74	16	4	6
	Tema/Accra–Bamako	80	9	5	6
Central Africa	Douala–N'Djaména	60	17	10	13
	Douala–Bangui	60	19	9	12
	Ngaoundéré–N'Djaména	53	11	14	22
	Ngaoundéré–Moundou	38	12	23	27
East Africa	Mombasa–Kampala	79	13	6	2
	Kampala–Kigali	67	31	1	1
Southern Africa	Lusaka–Johannesburg	51	48	1	0
	Lusaka–Dar-es-Salaam	60	38	1	1

Source: Trucking survey data and own calculations.

are significant for the few companies that finance their capital investments with bank credit or leasing (table 6.6).

In East Africa, fuel and lubricants represent the main variable costs.
High fixed costs for Kenyan truckers are largely explained by high costs
of staff, finance, and depreciation.

In Southern Africa, fuel and tires account for more than 90 percent of
the variable costs. Zambian truckers consider the high levels of domestic
fuel prices as their main impediment to capturing a larger share of the
north-south corridor market.

In West Africa, the situation is similar to that in Central Africa. Fuel and
lubricants account for the bulk of variable costs (more than 70 percent for
fuel). Bribes are equal to or higher than tires (bribes are up to 10 percent
of variable costs along the Tema/Accra–Bamako route). Fixed costs com-
prise mainly staff and depreciation.

These results are consistent with Oyer (2007). Indeed, he found that
fuel consumption, at 42 percent, is the biggest portion of total VOC for
heavy trucks in East Africa. Tire costs are the second largest component
of VOCs at 16 percent. Maintenance and parts costs were the second

Table 6.6   Fixed Costs in the Subregions
(percentage of total)

Corridor	Route gateway/ destination	Staff (% of total fixed costs)	Depreciation (% of total fixed costs)	Finance (% of total fixed costs)	Other[a] (% of total fixed costs)
West Africa	Tema/Accra– Ouagadougou	46	31	0	23
	Tema/Accra–Bamako	44	43	0	13
Central Africa	Douala–N'Djaména	35	33	15	17
	Douala–Bangui	28	26	25	21
	Ngaoundéré– N'Djaména	36	35	0	29
	Ngaoundéré– Moundou	38	34	1	27
East Africa	Mombasa–Kampala	27	20	15	38
	Kampala–Kigali	27	29	3	41
Southern Africa	Lusaka–Johannesburg	43	15	0	42
	Lusaka–Dar-es-Salaam	53	8	0	39

Source: Trucking survey data and own calculations.
a. Includes licenses costs, administrative costs, insurance, communication costs, security, and losses related to
crime and theft.

lowest among all the truck categories, which can be explained by the fleet age, low yearly mileage, and maintenance strategies.

The impact of fuel prices on transport costs should be assessed carefully. Indeed, in the case of Zambia almost 80 percent of the fuel price is related to taxes and levies, which means that up to 40 percent of total transport costs in Zambia are directly affected by its taxation policy (table 6.7).

Duties and surtaxes on tires and spare parts can have a major impact on VOCs. For instance, in Malawi, eliminating the 25 percent duty and the 17.5 percent surtax would reduce the retail cost of new tires by approximately 32 percent. A similar reduction in duty and surtax on parts could reduce their retail cost by 32 percent and reduce vehicle maintenance costs by approximately 25 percent (assuming a ratio of parts cost to labor cost of 3 to 1).

Licenses, taxes, and levies. In a competitive environment like Southern Africa, licenses, taxes, and levies may have a major impact on margins of trucking companies. For example, a Mozambican company entering Zimbabwe must pay a road-user charge (US$25 per 100 kilometer), an entry visa charge (US$30), an insurance charge (US$300, valid for three months), a carbon tax (US$30, valid for one month), and a guarantee (US$120, valid for one year)—a total of approximately US$125 per trip. In countries where margins are usually limited to 10 percent and the main cost factors (fuel costs and depreciation costs) are given, almost half of the margin for a round trip to Zimbabwe can be spent for a Mozambican trucker on various taxes and levies. In Zambia or the Democratic Republic of Congo, compulsory taxes and levies are even much higher (between

Table 6.7   Fuel Prices in Zambia
(per liter)

Costs	In US$	In percentage
Wholesale price	0.11	8.4
Transport margin	0.03	2.0
Terminal fee	0.05	3.8
Oil marketing company margin	0.06	4.6
Dealer margin	0.04	3.1
Margins and wholesale price	**0.29**	**21.8**
Road levy	0.20	15.0
Excise duty	0.59	45.0
Value added tax	0.23	17.5
Energy Regulatory Board fees	0.01	0.7
Taxes and levies	**1.02**	**78.2**
Total fuel price	**1.31**	

Source: Gesellschaft für Technische Zusammenarbeit (GTZ) for fuel prices in 2006. Interviews for the breakdown.

US$400 and US$700), which makes any trip to these countries for a Mozambican company unprofitable. This is an example of unnecessary segmentation of transport markets and limits competition, in this case from Mozambican companies.

Breakdown of Fixed Costs

Despite relatively low wages, staff costs remain the most important fixed costs. Moreover, depreciation costs are also a major component of fixed costs for most African trucking companies (in spite of the old fleet).

Truck prices. Table 6.8 shows the average prices of the last three vehicles purchased by the trucking companies and the truckers surveyed. Secondhand heavy trucks in Kenya cost more than in the other countries (approximately 70 percent more) because Kenyans buy relatively "new" secondhand vehicles.

Contrary to a widespread perception about the negative impact of high import tariffs on imported trucks, an analysis of most-favored-nation (MFN) tariffs for imported heavy trucks does not seem to corroborate this. Indeed, if we exclude South Africa and Zambia, import tariffs do not seem to explain why trucks are considered to be so expensive (see table 6.9). However, import tariffs may be complemented with other taxes such as value added tax (VAT) or environmental taxes, resulting in a similar tax burden as in South Africa and Zambia and maybe even higher. Moreover, some countries may in reality continue to impose tariffs that diverge from the regional harmonized tariff schedule. Consequently, a new truck costs three or four times as much as a used truck.

In an environment where truck utilization is low (40,000–60,000 kilometers) and transport prices are not extremely high, a trucker or trucking company cannot afford to purchase a new truck because there is

Table 6.8   Heavy Truck Prices
(current US$)

Country	New	Second hand
Burkina Faso	163,333	27,000
Ghana	113,333	24,688
Uganda[a]	93,000	30,690
Kenya	169,200	52,144
Zambia	n.a.	19,613

Source: Trucking survey data and own calculations.

a. Prices are lower because Ugandan truckers/trucking companies usually operate with smaller new trucks. But new trucks remain operated marginally by Ugandan truckers and trucking companies.

Table 6.9   Import Tariffs for Imported Trucks
(percentage of value of imports)

Country	MFN tariff	Year
Rwanda	5.00	2005
Cameroon	10.00	2005
Central African Republic	10.00	2005
Chad	10.00	2005
Niger	10.00	2006
Togo	10.00	2005
Burkina Faso	10.00	2006
Uganda	12.50	2006
Kenya	12.50	2006
South Africa	13.33	2006
Zambia	15.00	2003

Source: TRAINS, UNCTAD.
Note: Data for trucks over 20 metric tons of gross vehicle weight (HS 870423).

Table 6.10   Monthly Wage for Permanent Full-Time Truck Drivers
(in current US$)

Country	Median	Standard deviation	Maximum	Minimum
Burkina Faso	131.1	41.3	350.0	60.0
Ghana	193.0	82.8	420.0	70.0
Cameroon	217.4	65.8	400.0	100.0
Chad	189.0	56.9	400.0	100.0
Kenya	269.0	92.8	504.0	144.0
Uganda	162.5	42.9	240.0	72.0
Zambia	160.2	111.5	683.7	43.4

Source: Trucking survey data and own calculations.

a very high likelihood of defaulting on the loan. Truck prices then are a problem, but the operating environment is even more problematic. Indeed, where long-term direct contracting does not exist and margins can hardly reach US$20,000–30,000 per year, it becomes extremely risky to invest US$150,000 in a new truck. In a regulated environment, and when low allocated freight and bad connections with the freight allocation bureau are the case, there is absolutely no incentive to purchase a new truck, even if import tariffs are lowered.

Low wages. Truck drivers' wages are generally low in Sub-Saharan Africa (table 6.10). Wages in Kenya and Cameroon are the highest in the subregion, the most professional companies being located in East Africa. Some large companies have started to invest in truckers' training and have increased wages in order to keep trained drivers. In West Africa and Chad, wages remain lower because trained truckers and professional companies are almost nonexistent.

Company taxes. If we exclude Kenya, all the countries in the subregion show similar ratios of taxes to total VOCs (see table 6.11). In general, in a given country the trucking industry did not show clear deviation from all other industries as they all face the same burdens with respect to fixed costs.

Licenses. Table 6.12 shows diverse regulatory restrictions by country for operating or owning a vehicle. All the studied Sub-Saharan Africa countries require a license to operate vehicles, but not all countries require a license to own a vehicle (for example in Ghana). Impediments like waiting periods or requests for gifts or informal payments in order to get a license vary a lot across countries.

Table 6.11   Ratio of Company Taxes to Total Costs
(by truck, country, and type of industry)

Region	Country	Type of industry	Ratio of taxes to VOC (percent of total)
West Africa	Burkina Faso	All	4
		Trucking industry	3
		Truckers	5
	Ghana	All	1
		Trucking industry	1
		Truckers	1
Central Africa	Cameroon	All	5
		Trucking industry	4
		Truckers	5
	Chad	All	4
		Trucking industry	5
		Truckers	4
East Africa	Uganda	All	1
		Trucking industry	1
		Truckers	1
	Kenya	All	25[a]
		Trucking industry	25
		Truckers	26
Southern Africa	Zambia	All	2
		Trucking industry	2
		Truckers	—

Source: Trucking survey data and own calculations.

a. The very high taxes reported in the trucking survey for Kenya seem to correspond to a misunderstanding of the question since tax levels do not seem to be much higher than in the other countries studied.

Table 6.12 Licenses

Country	License needed before beginning operations (%)[a]		Number of days it takes to get the license	Gift or informal payment expected or requested in order to obtain the license (%)[b]
Burkina Faso	License to operate	**95**	22.7	24
	License to own vehicle	61	4.2	5
Ghana	License to operate	**90**	49.1	43
	License to own vehicle	19	100.3	23
Cameroon	License to operate	**99**	34.1	**60**
	License to own vehicle	**93**	8.8	35
Chad	License to operate	**99**	20.6	**89**
	License to own vehicle	**100**	15.2	**77**
Uganda	License to operate	76	5.7	5
	License to own vehicle	55	6.3	0
Kenya	License to operate	**100**	24.9	**66**
	License to own vehicle	**97**	26.4	**64**
Zambia	License to operate	**93**	49.8	7
	License to own vehicle	70	23.3	8

Source: Trucking survey data and own calculations.

a. The percentage represents the number of trucking industries/truckers that said YES to this question: Do you need a license to operate?

b. The percentage represents the number of trucking industries/truckers that said YES to this question: Was a gift/informal payment expected or requested in order to obtain a license?

Public Procedures and the Opportunity Cost of Delays

Procedures such as customs and personnel checks at border crossings influence truck utilization (see table 6.13). In Africa, there seems to be a strong positive correlation between transport prices and the number of cross-border operations.

Trucking companies in East Africa illustrate the opportunity cost of delays (at borders, weighbridges, and port). For many years, trucks have been waiting between one to two days at Malaba, the main border post between Kenya and Uganda. There are several reasons for the delays, including limited parking space for trucks, limited space in the customs yard, poor cargo documentation, and duplication of processes with Kenyan and Ugandan customs. Although some freight forwarders present documentation in advance of crossing, customs officials start to process documentation only when trucks have entered the customs yard, which usually takes several hours because of congestion and the reasons given above.

Table 6.13   Opportunity Cost of Delays

Country	Time to cross the border (hours)	Time waited to pick up freight once inside the port (hours)
Burkina Faso	**25.36**	**23.38**
	(14.9)	(12.2)
Ghana	**30.33**	**24.71**
	(31.3)	(23.1)
Cameroon	**26.55**	**12.38**
	(24.2)	(12.4)
Chad	**11.65**	**12.38**
	(15.2)	(12.4)
Uganda	**15.25**	**11.75**
	(15.9)	(8.1)
Kenya	**8.18**	**5.93**
	(7.2)	(1.32)
Zambia	**26.5**	**16.55**
	(26.0)	(20.6)

Source: Trucking survey data and own calculations.
Note: Figures are averages with standard deviation shown in parentheses.

Ugandan and Kenyan authorities are now working on establishing a joint border post, which should enable trucks to go through with only one stop instead of two. When fully implemented, this initiative should help decrease delays at the border dramatically.

In addition to border delays, weighbridge operations (for instance at Mariakani, Kenya, or at Mombasa port) also contribute to long delays along the northern corridor.

If all these delays (port, weighbridges, border) could be significantly reduced, vehicle yearly mileage should improve by at least 20,000 kilometers, which would help increase the ratio of a vehicle's capital utilization, thus reducing average yearly operating costs per vehicle and perhaps leading to transport price reductions.

In Southern Africa, delays at Beit Bridge or Chirundu border posts have a similar impact as those at Malaba in East Africa. Trucking companies waste several days at these border posts between South Africa and Zimbabwe and Zimbabwe and Zambia. For several years, authorities have been working on establishing a joint border post. These projects have not yet materialized, but important steps have been taken at Chirundu. Delays at Beit Bridge and Chirundu cost US$3.5 million each year to trucking companies only, which is equal to approximately a 25 percent surcharge on transport costs along the corridor.[5]

If all these delays (port, border) could be significantly reduced, vehicle yearly mileage should improve by at least 30,000 kilometers along the north-south corridor, which would help reduce operating costs and prices.

Notes

1. Variable costs include fuel, tires, maintenance, and bribes, whereas fixed costs include staff, licensing, administrative expenses, insurance, communication, security, losses, finance, and depreciation.

2. The average operating costs are calculated on a significantly large sample of trucks operating regularly on these routes: Douala–N'Djaména (35 observations), Douala–Bangui (18 observations), Ngaoundéré–N'Djaména (23 observations), and Ngaoundéré–Moundou (17 observations).

3. See chapter 7, table 7.1, on infrastructure condition and overload control by corridor.

4. In HDM-4, overhead, administrative costs, and bribes are not taken into account.

5. If we assume fixed costs of a six-axle truck (from the South African road freight association), 2.5 days' delay at Beit Bridge (Mthembu-Salter 2007), and 1.5 days' delay at Chirundu (FESARTA 2007), more than US$1,180 are lost for each trip in delays at border crossings. Traffic is assumed to be 500 trucks per day at Beit Bridge and 100 at Chirundu, with a conservative estimate of 25 turnarounds per year. Delays on the return trip are not estimated.

CHAPTER 7

The Impact of Road Conditions on Transport Costs

In Sub-Saharan Africa, most truck drivers and government officials blame poor roads for the high variable operating costs of the trucks. However, results from this study suggest that road conditions do not have a large negative impact on operating costs along the selected international corridors. This chapter analyzes the issue.

Road Conditions in the Study Corridors

Road conditions vary widely in the study corridors (table 7.1). For some routes, only 45 percent of the road is in good condition (Douala–N'Djaména); for others, the whole route is in good condition (one route in Central Africa and the two routes in South Africa).

How Road Conditions Affect Operating Costs

Roads in poor condition result in higher variable costs of operation because they (i) reduce fuel efficiency; (ii) damage the vehicles, leading to higher maintenance and higher operation costs; (iii) reduce the life of tires; (iv) reduce vehicle utilization because of lower speeds; and (v) reduce the life of the truck. How significant is the impact of poor roads on variable costs, and what factors make the impact bigger or smaller?

Table 7.1   Infrastructure Condition and Load Control

Region	Origin	Destination	Percentage of route in good and fair condition
West Africa	Tema/Accra	Ouagadougou	82
	Tema/Accra	Bamako	61
Central Africa	Douala	N'Djaména	45
	Douala	Bangui	53
	Ngaoundéré	Moundou	100
	Ngaoundéré	N'Djaména	61
East Africa	Mombasa	Kampala	86
	Kampala	Kigali	75
Southern Africa	Lusaka	Johannesburg	100
	Lusaka	Dar-es-Salaam	no data

Source: Task team calculations.
Note: Figures represent the percentage of the route that could be traveled at 50 km/hour in all seasons.

The trucking survey and HDM-4 simulations show mixed results. In two African subregions where traffic is low and truck fleets are old, as long as international corridor routes are paved and in fair condition road conditions do not emerge as a major hindrance to transport efficiency. However, on East Africa's main trade corridors, improving road conditions would have a significant impact on lowering transport costs, even if the roads are in fair condition to begin with.

Four variable costs usually are affected by road conditions: life of trucks, life of tires, maintenance costs, and fuel consumption. There are strategies that truckers can follow to reduce the impact of road conditions on operating costs:

- *Life of trucks*. Poor road conditions might shorten the operational life of trucks due to increased wear and tear. Although it is likely that this does take place, it is difficult to determine the respective share of causes such as suboptimal road condition, inadequate maintenance strategy, poor quality of parts and repair jobs, overloads, or other factors.
- *Life of tires.* Often the main reason the operational life of tires is shorter than expected is the use of low-quality tires to reduce the initial costs.[1]
- *Vehicle maintenance costs.*[2] Maintenance costs caused by poor roads do not impact significantly overall VOCs along international corridors. This is because maintenance costs rarely exceed 20 percent of total costs. It seems that costs are kept low by the owners' maintenance

strategy for old trucks. Sometimes preventive maintenance is delayed or even skipped altogether. On the other hand, old trucks also mean simple technology, which allows creative truckers to tinker with their engines and improvise repairs and parts, thus limiting maintenance costs. Truckers should use their knowledge of actual conditions to decide what type of truck to buy and which maintenance strategy is optimal.

- **Fuel consumption.** Like maintenance costs, fuel consumption is higher when road conditions are bad. However, the use of old, secondhand trucks may be a more critical factor for fuel consumption than road condition. As with tires and maintenance, truckers should use their knowledge of actual conditions to create an optimal strategy regarding truck fleet age and truck specifications.

Travel time is much shorter than it used to be, in large part because much road improvement has been carried out in Africa over past decades with the support of donors (mostly the European Union (EU) and the World Bank). Accessing the capital cities has become easier and faster. However, there are still a few road sections that require major improvements as well as some missing links to be built, notably in Central Africa.

Travel time between cities is not very dependent on the average speed at which a truck operates. More important than slow speed is the time a truck is idling while waiting for administrative procedures to be performed (at borders or at the terminals during loading or unloading). For instance, along the northern corridor in East Africa, truckers usually lose up to four hours in reduced speed because of poor road conditions along some segments, but they spend on average more than one day at the border crossing between Kenya and Uganda.

Apparently, the only road condition that has a significant impact on trip average speed is the congested exits to ports or major cities. These exits are found on routes such as Nairobi along the northern corridor or Yaoundé in Central Africa. Most African ports were built during colonial times with the city built around them, and exit routes are now in most cases inadequate.

Quantifying the impact of poor roads on transport costs. Tables 7.2–7.4 give approximate figures for the impact of road rehabilitation on VOCs using the HDM-4 model, with parameters of the model collected from the trucking survey. Estimates differ from the usual economic analyses of road projects for two reasons: (i) in almost all HDM-4 simulations, new truck prices are used, which inevitably inflates operating costs because of poor road condition; (ii) HDM-4 simulations assume high truck

Table 7.2   Unit Vehicle Operating Costs Savings from Road Improvement
(US$ per vehicle-year)

Road condition	West Africa	Central Africa	East Africa
Fair to good	3,163[a]	3,382	9,581
Poor to good	13,498	18,038	44,393

Source: Trucking survey data and own calculations.
a. Data are based on weighing figures on the share of new and secondhand trucks from the trucking survey.

Table 7.3   Vehicle Operating Costs Savings from Road Improvement
(US$ thousands per year)

Road condition	West Africa		Central Africa		East Africa	
	Minimal traffic[a]	*Maximal traffic*	*Minimal traffic*	*Maximal traffic*	*Minimal traffic*	*Maximal traffic*
Fair to good	158.2	474.5	169.1	507.3	1,916.2	6,706.7
Poor to good	674.9	2,024.7	901.9	2,705.7	8,878.6	31,075.1

Source: Trucking survey data and own calculations.
a. Minimal traffic corresponds to 50 trucks per day in West and Central Africa, 200 per day in East Africa (northern corridor), and maximum traffic corresponds to 150 trucks per day in West and Central Africa and 700 per day in East Africa.

Table 7.4   Indicative Internal Rate of Return of Infrastructure Rehabilitation
(percent)

Road condition	West Africa		Central Africa		East Africa	
	50 km project	*100 km project*	*50 km project*	*100 km project*	*50 km project*	*100 km project*
Fair to good						
Min. traffic	<0	<0	<0	<0	7	0
Max. traffic	<0	<0	<0	<0	30	15
Poor to good						
Min. traffic	<0	<0	<0	<0	38	20
Max. traffic	8	1	12	3	127	65

Source: Trucking survey data and own calculations.
Note: Assumptions are the following: savings are constant for 20 years for a 1,000 kilometer corridor, yearly traffic growth equal 3 percent, rehabilitation costs are US$500,000 per kilometer, road maintenance costs are excluded, and savings are discounted. We take into account only truck traffic.

utilization, which results in higher than real maintenance costs; in fact, truck utilization in Africa is much lower than assumed in the simulations.

Table 7.3 gives an approximate computation of the impact of road improvements using figures obtained from HDM-4 simulations.

Table 7.4 presents indicative results of the cost-benefit analysis of partial road rehabilitation on a given corridor of 1,000 kilometers, depending on changes in road condition.

In West and Central Africa, because of low traffic, low truck utilization, and old fleets, even if rehabilitation is limited to 50 kilometers of a road section in poor condition, the internal rate of return of the project is not positive (taking into account only the vehicle operating costs savings). On the contrary, in East Africa, in almost all cases, road rehabilitation is justified, mainly because of a relatively higher traffic volume (minimum traffic along the northern corridor—up to Kampala—is at least 200 trucks per day).

Tables 7.2–7.4 demonstrate that because of the high cost of road improvement and the relatively old fleets, rehabilitation on hundreds of kilometers of road would not be economically justified if traffic were less than 200 trucks per day. Below such traffic levels, rehabilitation probably should take place only when the road is in poor or very poor condition (and only if the benefit from VOCs reduction were passed on to the final user of transport services).

For roads with high traffic, such as routes along the northern corridor, a long-term investment plan probably should be developed in order to keep the corridor in at least fair condition.

Notes

1. Low-quality tires eventually translate into higher costs per kilometer. Still, truckers in Africa need to take into account both initial and replacement costs when making a decision on the purchase of tires.

2. It is worth noting that some maintenance costs could be inflated in reality because some drivers think of the costs of routine maintenance rather than the costs of infrequent major repairs. However, in general, maintenance costs remain marginal compared with fuel costs.

CHAPTER 8

The Trucking Market in Africa: Perceptions and Reality

The trucking survey helps clarify perception and reality regarding truckers' and trucking companies' views of the main factors influencing transport costs and prices. This understanding is useful for formulating and implementing trucking market reforms.

Two factors often mentioned as explanatory variables for the level of costs and prices are trade imbalance and thickness of the market. Regarding trade imbalance, the reality is that most companies are able to find return freight on the most important international corridors. Furthermore, countries with the most unbalanced trade flows, like Uganda, are able to get lower transport prices than Central African countries such as Cameroon and Chad (table 8.1).

The thinness or thickness of the market is probably not a major factor either, at least not compared to other factors such as the market competitiveness. The case of Zambia illustrates this point. Despite the fact that Zambia is a landlocked country and Cameroon a coastal country and that total traffic flows are lower in the former than in the latter, transport prices are much higher in Cameroon than in Zambia (table 8.2).

Data about trade imbalances and market thickness were discarded, or at least not taken seriously, by trucking companies and truckers surveyed for this study. Operators had a consensus that the main factors influencing

Table 8.1   Transport Prices and Trade Imbalance

	Uganda	Cameroon	Chad
Export/import imbalance (percent)	10	45	30
Average transport price (in U.S. cents per tkm)	8	10	11

Source: Ports data for exports/imports imbalance.

Table 8.2   Transport Prices and Trade Flows

	Zambia	Cameroon
Total traffic flows (in million metric tons per year)	4.1	6.1
Average transport price (in U.S. cents per tkm)	5–6	10

Source: Ports data for exports/imports imbalance.

their costs and prices were the price of fuel and the condition of roads. The actual impact of fuel prices and road conditions vary.

Fuel costs all over Africa are a legitimate concern inasmuch as they account for approximately 50 percent of total VOCs, a share that continues to grow with the surge in oil prices.

The impact of road conditions is less clear. Its perceived impact may be explained by the fact that answers to the survey do not seem to be well reasoned. For example, if road conditions were truly one of the main constraints for this industry, trucking companies and truckers should also be complaining about high vehicle maintenance and tire costs, because poor road conditions are known to increase maintenance costs. However, except in East Africa and in Ghana, concerns about road conditions are not linked with vehicle maintenance costs, which means that road condition may not be as critical as some truckers think (see table 8.3).

Moreover, truckers in Central Africa usually complain about the costs of corruption. The level of corruption is similar to that in West Africa, but it accounts for only a small fraction of operating costs. On the contrary, in East Africa, the perceived constraints seem to be very consistent with results of this study, probably because trucking professionalism is much higher than in Central and West Africa.

Equally interesting is that market regulation, freight allocation, and delays at the border were not identified as major constraints by truckers and heads of trucking companies. It is probably easy to explain this omission. The interviewed companies and truckers are beneficiaries of the current

Table 8.3   Main Perceived Constraints to the Trucking Industry
(percent)

Region	Country	1st obstacle	2nd obstacle	3rd obstacle
West Africa	Burkina Faso	Fuel cost, 98	Missing road links, 88	Road condition, 61
	Ghana	Fuel cost, 33	High maintenance cost, 27	Vehicle cost, 26
Central Africa	Cameroon	Fuel cost, 46	Road condition, 38	Corruption, 32
	Chad	Road condition, 76	Fuel cost, 72	Corruption, 70
East Africa	Kenya	Road condition, 87	Fuel cost, 54	High maintenance, 47
	Uganda	Fuel cost, 80	Road condition, 78	High maintenance, 62
Southern Africa	Zambia	Fuel cost, 66	Road condition, 36	Corruption, 36

Source: Trucking survey data and own calculations.

Table 8.4   Trucking Companies and Truckers Belonging to an Association
(percent)

Country	All	Trucking companies	Truckers
Burkina Faso	**66**	88	58
Ghana	**67**	53	71
Cameroon	36	76	25
Chad	**76**	86	74
Kenya	30	71	15
Uganda	39	65	32
Zambia	11	37	2

Source: Trucking survey data and own calculations.

system. They do not want more competition if some of them inevitably would be expelled from the market. In this regard, a proxy could be the membership of companies or truckers in a trucking association. It seems that in regulated environment, as in West and Central Africa, companies and truckers predominantly join a trucking association knowing that without this membership getting a load would be much more difficult. However, in a deregulated environment, as in East Africa, a membership is less important since sales depend on the individual professionalism of a company and not on being part of the existing system of cartels or truckers' association (see table 8.4).

CHAPTER 9

Assessment of Policy Options

The formulation of policy options requires policy makers to distinguish between a regulated and a more mature, competitive, and liberalized transport market:

- In a competitive environment with high traffic volumes, measures to improve road conditions and limit fuel prices are likely to yield significant results. Measures to reduce delays at borders or weighbridges would also help increase truck utilization.
- In a regulated environment, as in West and Central Africa, regulatory constraints (formal and informal) should be dismantled as they are the root cause of limited competition, poor service, and high transport prices.

This chapter analyzes policy options for West and Central Africa together because of the subregions' similarity. East and South Africa are analyzed separately because although their transport markets have similarities, there are differences in the impact of specific policies. In presenting policies, this chapter also includes feedback from stakeholders' workshops conducted in the four subregions. All four workshops were attended by a balanced representation of all major stakeholders involved with the road freight market and operations.

Policies for West and Central Africa

On the basis of the trucking survey data, this study assessed the possible impact of various transport policies and facilitation measures. The intention was to determine which policies or measures would most reduce transport costs and prices. Table 9.1 presents the expected approximate impact of the following measures: (i) road rehabilitation of the corridor from fair to good, (ii) 20 percent reduction in border delays, (iii) 20 percent reduction in fuel prices, and (iv) 20 percent reduction in informal payments. The expected impact varies among companies. The cost for carrying out the measures varies widely. Road rehabilitation, for example, is capital intensive and requires government funding, whereas a reduction in informal payments can be achieved at minimal or no cost to the government.

On transport costs, the most effective measures are likely to be a decrease in fuel costs, further road rehabilitation, and, to a lesser extent, reduction of border-crossing delays. The slight decrease in transport costs that improving the corridor would yield is an indicator that, irrespective of the impact of road improvement on prices, rehabilitation of the corridor may not be economically justified, either because the current road condition is good enough or the traffic level does not justify improvement, or both. On the contrary, despite the perceived effects of informal payments, reducing them by 20 percent would have a marginal impact on transport costs.[1]

The crucial point is that such measures have no impact on reducing transport prices. Indeed, without competition, truckers and trucking companies are likely to capture the reduction in costs and translate them into higher profits rather than lower prices. Consequently, where cartels still

Table 9.1   Expected Impact of Policies in a Regulated Environment
(percent)

Measures	Decrease in transport costs	Increase in sales	Decrease in transport price
Rehabilitation of corridor from fair to good	−5	..	+/−0
20% reduction of border-crossing time	−1	+2/+3	+/−0
20% reduction of fuel price	−9	..	+/−0
20% reduction of informal payment	−1	..	+/−0

Source: Trucking survey data and own calculations.
Note: For the simulation, VOC data from the Tema/Accra–Ouagadougou corridor were used.
.. Negligible (these items are unlikely to induce more turnarounds and then more sales).

prevail as in West and Central Africa, they should be dismantled because they prevent measures that would help the trucking industry reduce transport costs, needless to say transport prices.

Truckers in West and Central Africa may argue that currently there is competition, sometimes strong, in the transport market. The trucking survey shows, however, that whenever competition does exist, it is not based on price and quality of service, but on the capacity to circumvent the rules and capture loads with little or no negotiation on prices or services quality. Thus, creating a true, strong competitive environment is essential to reducing prices.

Deregulating the trucking industry in West and Central Africa. Breaking the regulatory status quo in many countries is difficult due to a coalition of interests opposing change. For example, truckers have strong leverage with high-level authorities who can block trade. This is the case because, in Africa, the trucking corridors under review often are the main, and sometimes the only, transport mode for international and domestic trade. Furthermore, governance problems occur in the trucking industry because some high-level authorities own or indirectly control trucks or trucking companies. These authorities benefit from the status quo and market-sharing schemes.

Deregulating the trucking industry in West and Central Africa is less a technical than a political and social issue. The main concern is the potential large decrease in the number of truckers. Participants in the stakeholders' workshops in Ouagadougou and Bangui strongly emphasized the importance of mitigating the social impact that would result from a more efficient but reduced trucking industry. The coalition of interests in most West and Central African countries might not resist reforms as long as compensation schemes are introduced with the purpose of paying, at least partly, for the social costs of such reforms.

Fiscal incentives could be put in place to obtain the support of stakeholders for market deregulation. Such incentives should aim at encouraging a maximum utilization of trucks. This is not the case today because truckers pay the brunt of taxes through fuel. This high fuel tax favors underused trucks, which pay tax only when moving.

One possible reform is to convert the majority of tax revenue collected through fuel (variable costs) into truck ownership and registration taxes (fixed costs). For truckers, this change would be a major tax increase for operators who put less mileage on their trucks, but a significant saving for those with higher mileage—higher-efficiency truckers. The tax change would be fiscally neutral above a given level of truck utilization

(100,000 kilometers per year, for instance). Such a change in the taxation structure of the trucking activities would favor good performers and thus encourage a major structural change.

A queuing system would then be unable to protect low performers while encouraging all others to bypass it to access loads. Finally, the *tour de rôle* would disappear. Such a reform would be relatively politically easy (as all other road users would benefit from lower fuel taxes) but complex to design (as it would need a thorough review of a major component of the fiscal system to ensure good balance between revenue collection and transport policy targets). It might also be difficult to implement as the collection of high license fees would be a potential source of corruption.

Another possible and simpler fiscal reform would be to tax imports of trucks, not as a proportion of their purchase costs, but as a lump sum. If high enough, this tax would favor the purchase of more expensive, more reliable trucks. This would in turn increase the fixed costs share in total costs and therefore encourage higher use of the truck fleet. Such a reform might also result in a net increase in fiscal revenues for governments. In the current situation, new, expensive trucks are not imported at all, and therefore the import tax revenue coming from new trucks is almost zero. In addition, taxes on old, imported trucks do not generate much revenue.

Even in a case where balancing fiscal revenue is not an issue, countries' policy on importing old vehicles should be reviewed in light of vehicle safety and extra pollution emission from aged vehicles. Some measures could be put in place to encourage import of "relatively young" second-hand trucks or to penalize the import of older ones. In such cases, import tariffs could be used not as a fiscal revenue generation target, but as a tool to control imports, as long as enforcement of such measures from customs administrations seems possible. For example, a country could set a target for import of secondhand trucks no older than eight years of age. It either could put a total ban on import of trucks more than eight years old, or it could progressively levy import tariffs for those who brought in trucks older than eight years. In sum, the study recommends a good review of secondhand truck import policy in Africa as it has implications for transport costs, in addition to road safety and the climate change agenda.

Stakeholders' workshops feedback. Workshops conducted for West and Central Africa[2] focused on the study's conclusion that without a liberalization of the transport market, measures reducing transport costs would not lower transport prices. The stakeholders, notably the trucking companies and owner-operators, accepted the findings of the study but were concerned that appropriate compensation schemes should be developed to mitigate the effects of the reform on the operators who would have to exit the road transport market. Participants strongly emphasized the importance of mitigating the social impact that would result from a streamlining of the transport sector on international corridors.

Further research and analysis will be needed to define in detail the possible compensation schemes to put in place so that some truckers exit the regional road transport market.

Policies for East Africa

The same policies or measures assessed in the highly regulated environment of West and Central Africa were tested in the deregulated environment of East Africa. The results are shown in table 9.2.

On costs, the most effective measures are likely to be road rehabilitation, reduction in fuel costs, and, to a lesser extent, reduction of border-crossing delays. Reducing informal payments would have a marginal impact on transport costs and prices. The higher impact of road rehabilitation and a drop in fuel prices in this region, compared with West and Central Africa, is explained by the higher volume of traffic and the bigger, more modern trucks in East Africa.

Reduced transport costs in East Africa are likely to translate into a reduction in transport prices, thanks to the deregulated market environment and contrary to the situation in West and Central Africa. Thus, such measures bring benefits throughout the economy, and can lead to a decrease in consumer prices. That is why it would be fully justified to invest in road rehabilitation on the major road corridors[3] and to seek ways

Table 9.2   Expected Impact of Policies in East Africa
(percent)

Measures	Decrease in transport costs	Increase in sales	Decrease in transport price
Rehabilitation of corridor from fair to good	−15	..	−7/−10
20% reduction of border-crossing time	−1/−2	+2/+3	−2/−3
20% reduction of fuel price	−12	..	−6/−8
20% reduction of informal payment	−0.3	..	+/−0

Source: Trucking survey data and own calculations.
Note: For the simulation, VOC data from the corridor Mombasa–Kampala were used.
.. Negligible (these items are unlikely to induce more turnarounds and then more sales).

to reduce fuel prices. Measures to reduce border delays should also be a priority and would help decrease transport prices.

Public authorities should scrutinize the efficiency of weighbridge operations in order to limit delays. Finally, transporters should be encouraged to use trucks with lower operating costs.

Stakeholders' workshop feedback. The stakeholders agreed with the findings of the study and proposed specific additions on a country basis:

- **Kenya/Uganda**
  - Implement the one-stop border post in Malaba (a key point in the economics of trucking in East Africa) while taking care of the infrastructure needs and minimized procurement. An extension of the status of "authorized economic operators" to several companies should lead to a reduction in waiting time at the Uganda–Kenya border.
  - Introduce along the northern corridor simplified documentation requirements as stated in the northern corridor Transport and Transit Agreement in order to reduce delays.
  - Establish a long-term investment plan to ensure that the Mombasa–Kampala corridor remains at least in fair condition in the medium and long term.
- **Kenya**
  - Review and probably lift the customs regulation that prohibits trucks from taking backloads in Kenya as this rule severely affects transport service costs along the northern corridor.
- **Uganda**
  - Review taxes on fuel and study the possibility of introducing a road fund levy within the limit of the existing level of taxation on fuel.

Policies for Southern Africa

The same measures assessed in the highly regulated environment of West and Central Africa were tested in the deregulated environment of Southern Africa. The results are shown in table 9.3.

The most effective measures are likely to be a reduction in fuel costs, increased road rehabilitation, and a reduction of border-crossing delays. Reducing informal payments would have a marginal impact on transport costs and prices. The higher impact of road rehabilitation and fuel price changes in this region, compared with West and Central Africa, is explained by the higher volumes of traffic and the larger and more modern fleet.

Table 9.3   Expected Impact of Policies in Southern Africa
(percent)

Measures	Decrease in transport costs	Increase in sales	Decrease in transport price
Rehabilitation of corridor from fair to good	–3/5	..	–2/–3
20% reduction of border-crossing time	–3/4	+18	–10/–15
20% reduction of fuel price	–10	..	–5/–7
20% reduction of informal payment	–1	..	+/–0

Source: Trucking survey data and own calculations.
Note: For the simulation, VOC data from the north-south corridor were used (using Zambia operators' data).
.. Negligible (these items are unlikely to induce more turnarounds and then more sales).

The reduction in transport costs in Southern Africa, thanks to its deregulated market environment and contrary to the situation in West and Central Africa, is likely to translate into a reduction in transport prices, especially in the case of lower fuel costs or smaller border-crossing delays.

Measures to reduce border delays should be a top priority in Southern Africa as they are much higher than in East Africa (the crossings at Beit Bridge and Chirundu take a minimum of four days, which is at least twice as long as the Malaba crossing in East Africa). Reducing such delays, taking into account the high fixed cost of the Southern African trucking operators, would significantly help improve utilization of the fleet and staff and would lower transport prices.

Stakeholders' workshop feedback. As in East Africa, stakeholders agreed with the findings of the study and proposed specific additions on a country basis:

- **North-South Corridor (South Africa/Zambia/Zimbabwe)**
  - Implement the one-stop border-post principle (especially for Beit Bridge and Chirundu border crossings) along the north-south corridor.
  - Prepare and sign as soon as possible, taking into account the strong political will to facilitate trade along the corridor and the work undertaken by a consultant, a trilateral agreement to create a Corridor Management Institution along the corridor. This institution should be financially sustainable and based on a cost recovery principle whereby road users pay for the operation costs of the corridor management facilities.

- Review the implementation of bilateral transport agreements, road-user charges guidelines, and levies and taxes paid at border crossings.
  - Support a strong technical link between donors, authorities, and the Southern African Development Community (SADC) Secretariat (through the trade and transport panel of experts).
- **Zambia**
  - Review taxes on fuel.
- **South Africa**
  - Review procedures at the main international border crossings.

Notes

1. However, if roadblocks induce significant transport unpredictability, nontransport logistics costs may increase exponentially and have a major impact on transport and logistics. See Arvis et al. (2007) for more details.

2. Workshops were carried out in Bangui for Central Africa in January 2008 and in Ouagadougou for West Africa in February 2008.

3. As Oyer (2007) points out, some sections of the northern corridor road could be realigned to shorten the distance traveled and reduce repeated gear changes. This would lower VOCs by reducing fuel and tire consumption.

CHAPTER 10

Implications for Economic and Fiscal Analysis and for Data Collection

The study findings suggest areas where countries should consider reviewing various approaches to economic analysis for transport investment, as well as data collection in areas related to transport and trucking. In particular, countries should work to improve the quality of economic analysis of road investments, the effectiveness of fiscal policies, and the monitoring of the road freight market.

Finance Regular Studies of Transport Prices and Costs Determinants

Data collection on the trucking fleet, transport prices, and costs is largely inadequate in most countries in Sub-Saharan Africa. For instance, data on vehicle registration have to be used with caution as many vehicles out of service have not been removed from the database. Vehicle registration data need to be systematically updated. Hard data on overloading practices are not available for most corridors in Africa despite the fact that major rehabilitation works of road infrastructure have been carried out or are under way and overloading practices should have been monitored and controlled in parallel to the new investment.

A good knowledge of market structure, regulation, and practices is critical to identify measures likely to bring the most benefits to the end users of transport services.

Improve the Economic Analysis of Road Projects

Better identification of interventions that lower the price end users pay for trucking services is crucial. In some regions, interventions targeted at increasing competition rather than improving paved roads are likely to be the most cost effective.

Economic analysis is the key tool for decisions on road investment and maintenance strategies. In most African countries and elsewhere in the developing world, investment in road projects and the design of maintenance strategies is done using the HDM-4 model, which requires data specific to the country of the analysis, including statistics on the country's trucking industry. However, such data are often unavailable, or only a small part of the data required is actually collected through the country's statistical systems. In the absence of country-specific data, analysts make use of data from other countries that they hope reflects the condition in the country of analysis. However, such data may be significantly different, thus affecting the results obtained with the HDM-4.

One problem with inputting trucking data is that the HDM-4 model assumes that truckers buy new trucks when they renew their fleets. The HDM-4 analysis should be improved knowing that in many African countries, truckers, especially those who operate on low-traffic roads, usually buy aged, secondhand trucks, at prices substantially below new trucks. Those low-priced vehicles are likely to benefit less from road improvements, which reduce the vehicle maintenance benefits that are part of the model. The HDM-4 model cannot deal with large fleets of secondhand vehicles, which are, however, the most common in Africa.

Although this study focused only on international corridors, it can suggest more broadly that for national corridors and local roads a return to economic analysis of road investments should be reviewed to better understand the impact of roads, especially rural roads,[1] on accessibility. This would include a better assessment of roads' development impact, both social and economic, and a better way to quantify the benefits of savings in travel time. The trucking survey and other literature suggest that such a return could lead to a better way of assessing the benefits of road improvements.

Numerous studies demonstrate that rural roads substantially promote social and economic development; the question is how best to assess the benefits and carry out economic analysis of rural road investments. This is especially important for low-volume rural roads, where improvement significantly increases mobility and creates new opportunities for development and access to markets and social services.

In addition, the impact of improved, low-cost rural roads in reducing transport time is not adequately captured in current economic decision models such as the Roads Economic Decision model (RED, a simpler version of the HDM-4). A study (Pedersen 2001) shows that 4 percent of total transport distance (rural and local trucking transport) contributes to almost 50 percent of total transport costs from Ghana to Europe. Rural transport is almost 500 times more expensive than maritime transport in U.S. dollars per ton-kilometer. The same study shows that reducing rural transport time by 50 percent would reduce total transport costs by almost 15 percent (table 10.1). Because investments on the main international corridors remain the major share of transport investments in Sub-Saharan Africa, this survey, combined with other surveys of investments on rural roads, could prove a milestone for road investment policy in the region.

It is possible, subject to more detailed study, that revisions of the road economic analysis along the lines suggested above may lead to important

Table 10.1   Transport Costs for Cocoa Beans from the Field in Ghana to Europe

	Operation	Transported distance (km)	Price (US$ per ton)	Share of total transport costs (%)	Price (U.S. cents/ ton-km)	Transport time of one ton (days)
Rural transport	Cocoa field to collection point	9	30	**25**	333.3	**25.0**
Trucking transport	From collection point to port	300	27	**23**	3.0	**0.3**
Handling	Reloading at depot		8	**7**		
Terminal handling	Handling at the port		10	**8**		
Ocean shipping		7,435	43	**37**	0.7	**0.9**
Total		7,744	118	**100**		

Source: Pedersen (2001).

changes in the composition of the road investment portfolio, giving more importance to secondary networks and rural access. Indeed, solving access problems in Africa remains vital for supporting both pro-growth and pro-poor policies. Such problems are directly linked to transport infrastructure and involve the allocation of significant financial resources to the maintenance and rehabilitation of existing national roads (secondary and tertiary roads) and to the expansion and rehabilitation of the secondary network and rural networks.

Assess the Impact of Fiscal Policies on Transport Services

Fiscal policies interact with transport services in several ways, but two are especially important: (i) fuel taxes and (ii) tariffs on the importation of vehicles, notably trucks. These policies are important because they significantly affect transport prices and the efficiency of the trucking industry.

Fuel taxes in practically all countries are the instrument of choice for recovering road maintenance costs from road users while generating revenue. As such, fuel taxes are both a user charge and a general tax. The impact of fuel taxes on transport costs and prices in Africa is substantial. On this continent, fuel costs amount to at least 40 percent of total VOCs, of which taxes amount to at least 50 percent. This means that at least 20 percent (and up to 40 percent) of VOCs are the result of fiscal policy. Because fuel taxes generally create less economic distortion than other taxes and are easy and inexpensive to collect, it is unlikely that governments will consider lowering fuel taxes and losing revenue.

However, in some countries, under some conditions, there may be a case for at least reviewing the level of the fuel tax. This would apply especially to some landlocked countries where the fuel tax is already high enough to recover road maintenance costs and generate additional revenues as a general tax. In such countries, where transport distances and crossing of the coastal country are significant trade barriers, the impact of fuel taxes on transport prices may be another critical factor hampering trade. Thus, there is a trade-off, usually neglected, between fiscal policies and truck competitiveness that needs to be carefully assessed. Furthermore, fuel prices at the pump in the landlocked country are significantly higher than those in the coastal country. In this case, creating a level playing field for the competition between the trucking industries of the landlocked and the coastal country would require lowering the price of fuel at the pump in the landlocked country. Zambia and Uganda are good examples of this situation. In Zambia, a 15 percent fuel levy comprises 10 percent of total

VOCs. Therefore, a drastic decrease of the fuel levy in Zambia could lead to a reduction of VOCs by no less than 4 percent.

Tariffs on truck imports are another dimension of the overlap between fiscal policies and transport. Such a tariff, depending on how it is set and structured, may have a major influence on the efficiency of the trucking industry and on the extent that road improvement programs benefit the trucking industry. There are two aspects to consider: the relative import tax between new and old trucks and the level of the tax. As this study has shown, the trucking fleet in most of Africa is old and inefficient. In most countries, the tariff on truck imports is a proportion of the truck price, and therefore lower for used, cheap trucks. Old trucks not only are fuel inefficient, but also create concerns on road safety hazard and pollution. Because of their inefficiency, they usually put on less annual mileage and thus do not benefit as much from road improvement as do newer trucks. Various alternative tariff policies could influence the truckers' decision regarding new versus old trucks. One policy would be a higher tariff (as a percentage of price) on secondhand trucks, relative to the age of trucks. Another could be a tariff set as a fixed lump sum, independent of the truck price, which would have the effect of favoring the import of newer trucks (as long as the trucking industry is deregulated in order to give an incentive to the most efficient companies to invest in new trucks).

Note

1. Incorporating social benefits into HDM-4 analysis remains a challenge. Furthermore, for low-volume roads (fewer than 50 vehicles per day), HDM-4 is not considered appropriate, and the cost-effectiveness approach is recommended.

CHAPTER 11

Conclusions, Recommendations, and the Role of International Development Agencies

Key Findings and Conclusions

This study measured the level of costs and prices and disaggregated them into three tiers: (i) VOCs, (ii) overall transport costs, and (iii) the transport price paid by end users. The study identified factors that cause high transport prices in Sub-Saharan Africa, analyzed the differences in the cost and price structure among the four subregions, and produced recommendations to lower transport prices. The study's main findings and conclusions are summarized in this chapter.

Key Findings

Our key findings are as follows:

- There is a substantial disconnect between transport costs and prices in numerous African countries. For example, transport costs in Africa are not abnormally high, whereas transport prices are high along some corridors, indicating a strong seller's market.
- Despite many poor efficiency factors (low yearly vehicle utilization rate, aging vehicle fleet, unbalanced trade . . .), trucking companies in Africa can still charge high prices and have relatively large profit margins along some corridors.

- Market regulation is an eminent price determinant. It hinders efficiency improvements in the trucking industry and stifles competitiveness, leading to high transport prices in Africa.
- The poor condition of road infrastructure might not necessarily be a critical factor for high transport costs.
- Age of the truck fleet and low utilization of vehicles seem to be significant determinants for transport costs, especially in West and Central Africa.

Conclusions

The trucking industry in West and Central Africa is characterized by cartels offering high prices and low service quality. In East Africa, the trucking environment is more competitive and the market more mature. The main transport corridors in Southern Africa are the most advanced in terms of efficiency, competitive prices, and service quality.

In West and Central Africa, there is a strong disconnect between transport costs and prices. Transport costs are not abnormally high, but transport prices are, suggesting the existence of a strong seller's market. In these subregions, despite poor efficiency in the operations, reflected by low truck utilization rates and aging vehicle fleets, trucking operators can charge high prices and have relatively large profit margins. This is possible because the cartels control the supply of transport services. Although in theory there is open entry to the road freight market, in practice the cartels make it almost impossible for new entrants to gain access to freight. It is possible to identify measures that will produce some reduction of transport costs, such as lowering fuel prices, but because of the self-regulated trucking market, reducing transport costs does not lower prices.

In East and Southern Africa, measures to improve road conditions and reduce fuel prices or delays at border posts help lower transport costs, but the two regions differ as to the level of impact of policy measures on costs, and more so on prices.

Poor condition of the road infrastructure may not be the most critical factor behind transport prices. This is a major finding since much road investment in Sub-Saharan Africa has been predicated on the assumptions that better roads lower transport costs and that truckers' cost savings are passed on to consumers as lower transport prices. The study finds these assumptions are far from accurate where the market is strongly regulated or where a cartel captures the benefits of road improvement.

The trucking industry in some landlocked countries of East Africa is placed at a competitive disadvantage because fuel prices at the pump in neighboring coastal countries are not as high, allowing their trucking companies to benefit from lower operating costs.

More broadly, the study has identified the need to review the approaches to economic analysis of road projects, the impact of taxation policies on the transport market, and the need to regularly update data on the trucking industry.

Recommendations

The study's key recommendation is to initiate institutional changes. Rent-seeking behavior and governance of the trucking industry are at the core of the issues faced by many low-income African countries. Without increased competition and successfully liberalizing trucking services where regulation remains strong, transport prices will remain high, service quality will not improve, and road users will not reap all the benefits of costly investments in infrastructure rehabilitation.

Deregulating the trucking industry in West and Central Africa would be the first critical undertaking toward the positive institution and policy adjustment. However, there would also be many negative impacts from this major policy adjustment. A serious mitigating plan should be in place to minimize the effects of introducing competition, including a reduction in the number of trucking operators. Deregulation should also facilitate new entrants' access to freight. A first step would be the abolition of cartels. A next step could be changes in the tax structure to reward those who operate more modern vehicles and utilize them more intensively.

In East Africa, improvement of some critical road sections in the corridor where the investment is economically justified will lead to lower transport costs and transport prices. The same would happen in the Southern Africa road network, although the corridor road considered in this study is in good condition and thus would receive limited benefit from improvement. On the other hand, creation of one-stop border posts would help reduce delays in border crossing and would lead to significant reduction of transport prices, especially in Southern Africa.

In East Africa, there may be a case for lowering fuel taxes in landlocked countries where the price of fuel at the pump is high relative to the pump price in neighboring coastal countries, thus handicapping the domestic trucking operators. A potential review of fuel taxes has to account for the fiscal impact and the need to ensure that fuel taxes actually are spent on road maintenance.

Studies should be carried out at the country level to assess (i) the specific situation of the trucking industry, (ii) the countries' taxation policy affecting fuel, and (iii) vehicle imports and their implications for transport costs and prices. Studies are also needed to look into ways and means to operationalize the findings presented in this report.

The Role of Development Partners

International development agencies, including the World Bank, should be encouraged to adapt their strategies in support of trade and transport on Africa's main international transport corridors in a way that maximizes the effect of their interventions. Transport services have been neglected for years on the assumption that reduction in VOCs would automatically lower transport prices. A better identification of interventions that lower the price of transport is essential so that they benefit the economy at large rather than a group of transport providers.

Where the appropriate intervention is to support the deregulation of the transport market, development agencies should provide technical assistance and help fund any compensation schemes required to mitigate the social effects of deregulation. Without coordinated efforts from the donor community, changes in regulation are unlikely to be implemented. Successful institutional change such as trucking deregulation requires patience, policy dialogue, and support from the donor community.

This study has identified the need to review the economic analysis of road projects and to assess the impact of fiscal policies on the transport market. It has also identified the need for countries to regularly update trucking data. The development agencies are well positioned to support this work by financing at the country level the review of relevant fiscal policies and the data collection, as well as refining the current methods of economic analysis of projects so as to facilitate a more effective investment decision.

Map 1. African Landlocked Countries

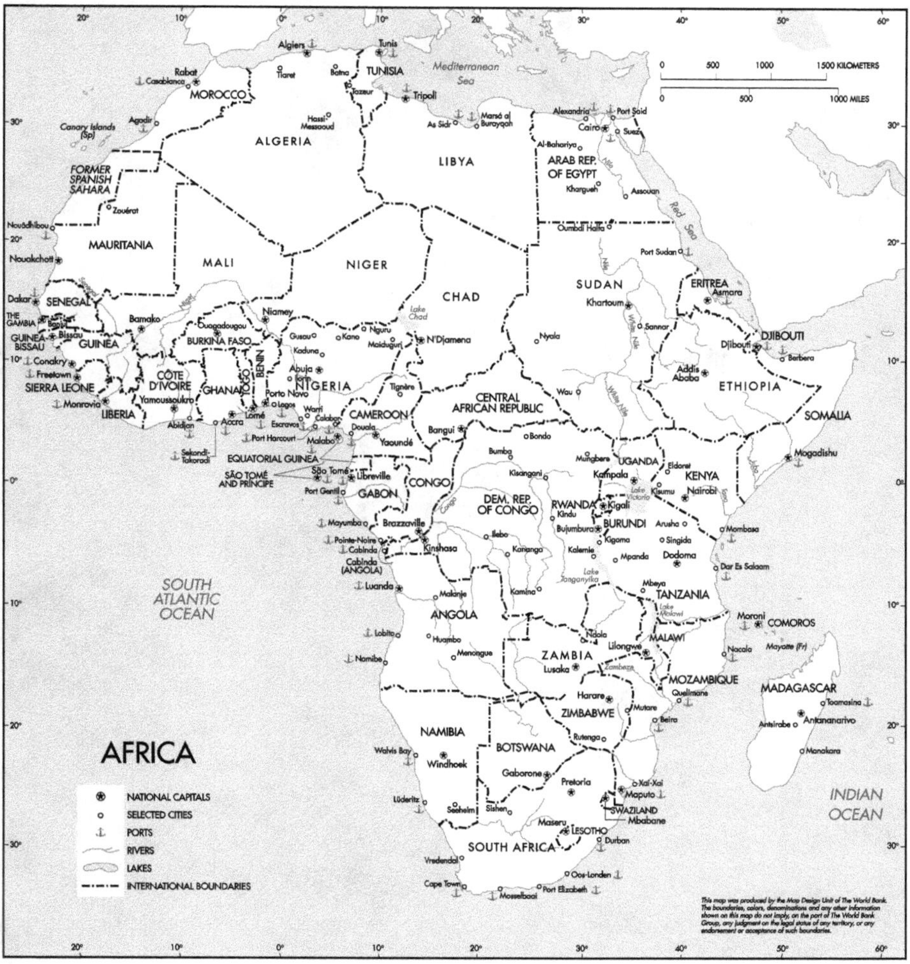

AFRICA

- ⊛ NATIONAL CAPITALS
- ○ SELECTED CITIES
- ⚓ PORTS
- ∿ RIVERS
- ◯ LAKES
- –·–·– INTERNATIONAL BOUNDARIES

MOROCCO
ALGERIA
LIBYA
ARAB REP. OF EGYPT
FORMER SPANISH SAHARA
MAURITANIA
MALI
NIGER
CHAD
SUDAN
ERITREA
DJIBOUTI
ETHIOPIA
SOMALIA
SENEGAL
THE GAMBIA
GUINEA-BISSAU
GUINEA
SIERRA LEONE
LIBERIA
CÔTE D'IVOIRE
BURKINA FASO
GHANA
BENIN
NIGERIA
CAMEROON
CENTRAL AFRICAN REPUBLIC
EQUATORIAL GUINEA
SÃO TOMÉ AND PRINCIPE
GABON
CONGO
DEM. REP. OF CONGO
UGANDA
KENYA
RWANDA
BURUNDI
TANZANIA
ANGOLA
Cabinda (ANGOLA)
ZAMBIA
MALAWI
COMOROS
MOZAMBIQUE
MADAGASCAR
ZIMBABWE
NAMIBIA
BOTSWANA
SWAZILAND
LESOTHO
SOUTH AFRICA

Mediterranean Sea
Red Sea
SOUTH ATLANTIC OCEAN
INDIAN OCEAN
Lake Chad
Lake Victoria
Lake Tanganyika
Lake Nyasa
Lake Malawi
White Nile
Blue Nile
Zambezi

Algiers, Tunis, Tiaret, Batna, TUNISIA, Tazeur, Tripoli, Rabat, Casablanca, Agadir, Canary Islands (Sp), Hassi Messaoud, As Sidr, Marsá al Burayqah, Alexandria, Port Said, Cairo, Suez, Al-Bahariya, Khargah, Aswan, Nouadhibou, Zouérat, Nouakchott, Oumdat Halfa, Port Sudan, Dakar, Bamako, Niamey, Nguru, Kano, Maiduguri, N'Djamena, Nyala, Khartoum, Sannar, Asmara, Djibouti, Berbera, Conakry, Freetown, Ouagadougou, Gusau, Kaduna, Abuja, Tignère, Wau, Addis Ababa, Mogadishu, Monrovia, Yamoussoukro, Abidjan, Accra, Lomé, Porto Novo, Lagos, Warri, Calabar, Douala, Yaoundé, Bangui, Maroua, Kisangani, Eldoret, Kampala, Kisumu, Nairobi, Sekondi-Takoradi, Escravos, Malabo, Bumba, Libreville, Port Gentil, Bondo, Kindu, Kigali, Bujumbura, Arusha, Mombasa, Mayumba, Brazzaville, Ilebo, Kigoma, Singida, Pointe-Noire, Cabinda, Kinshasa, Kananga, Kalemie, Mpanda, Dodoma, Dar Es Salaam, Luanda, Malanje, Kamina, Mbeya, Lobito, Huambo, Ndola, Lilongwe, Nacala, Moroni, Mayotte (Fr), Namibe, Menongue, ZAMBIA, Lusaka, Harare, Quelimane, Beira, Antsirabe, Antananarivo, Toamasina, Walvis Bay, Windhoek, Gaborone, Pretoria, Butenga, Mutare, Manakara, Lüderitz, Seeheim, Sishen, Xai-Xai, Maputo, Mbabane, Maseru, Durban, Vredendal, Vredendaal, Cape Town, Mosselbaai, Oos-London, Port Elizabeth

This map was produced by the Map Design Unit of The World Bank. The boundaries, colors, denominations and any other information shown on this map do not imply, on the part of The World Bank Group, any judgment on the legal status of any territory, or any endorsement or acceptance of such boundaries.

0 500 1000 1500 KILOMETERS
0 500 1000 MILES

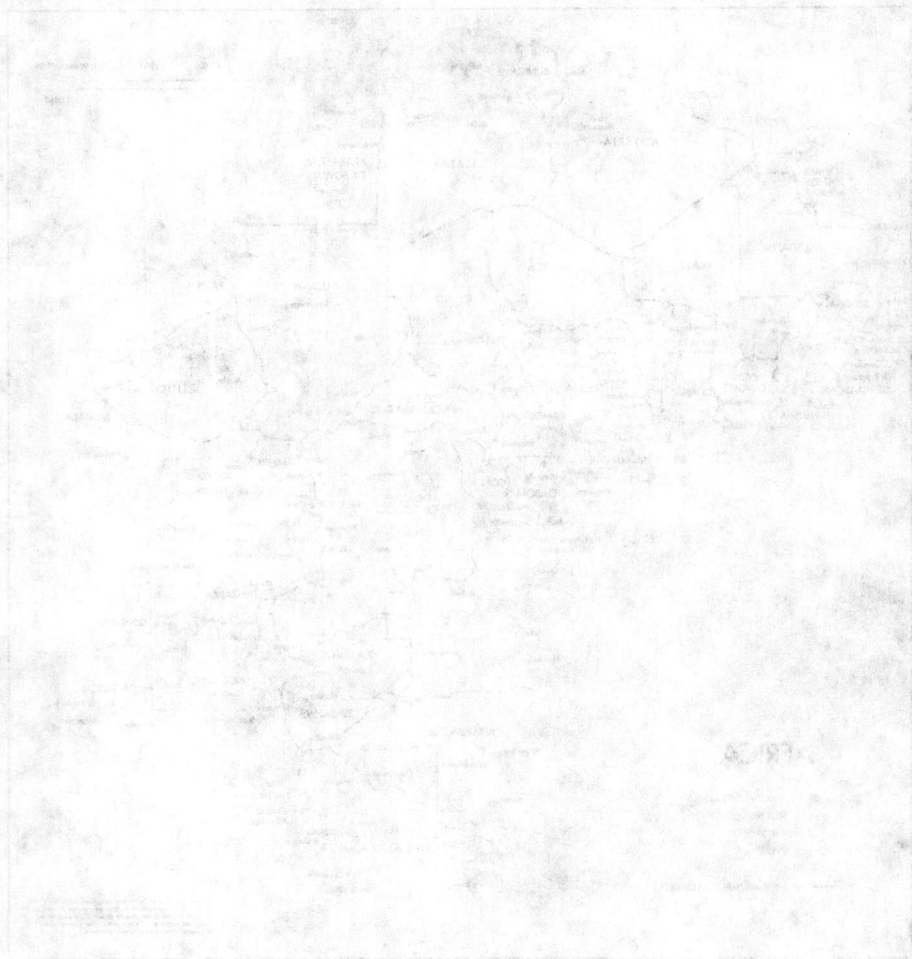

References

Adoléhoumé, A. 2007. "Analyse des Facteurs de Coûts et Prix de Transport en Afrique de l'Ouest: Cas du Niger." Unpublished paper, World Bank, Washington, DC.

Amjadi, A., and A. J. Yeats. 1995. "Have Transport Costs Contributed to the Relative Decline of Sub-Saharan African Exports?" Policy Research Working Paper No. 1559, World Bank, Washington, DC.

Arvis, J. F., G. Raballand, and J. F. Marteau. 2007. "The Cost of Being Landlocked: Logistics Costs and Supply Chain Reliability." Policy Research Working Paper No. 4258, World Bank, Washington, DC.

Chasomeris, M. 2005. "South Africa's Maritime Policy and Transformation of the Shipping Industry." Presentation at the 2005 Economic Society of South Africa. http://www.essa.org.za/download/papers2005.htm.

Comité National Routier (CNR). 2005. "Le Transport Routier de Marchandises en République Tchèque." Les Cahiers de l'Observatoire 222.

———. 2008. "Transport Routier de Marchandises et Coûts de Personnel de Conduite aux Pays-Bas." http://www.cnr.fr/e-docs/00/00/01/EB/document_etudes_cnr.phtml.

Council for Scientific and Industrial Research (CSIR), 2006. Annual State of Logistics Survey for South Africa. http://www.csir.co.za/Built_environment/pdfs/SOL2006.pdf.

Darbéra, R. 1998. "Measuring the Benefits from Road Haulage Deregulation: Example of Some French Results." Contribution to proceedings of the World Conference on Transport Research, Antwerp.

Dutz, M. 2005. "Road Freight Logistics, Competition and Innovation: Downstream Benefits and Policy Implications." Policy Research Working Paper No. 3768, World Bank, Washington, DC.

Dutz, M., A. Hayri, and P. Ibarra. 2000. "Regulatory Reform, Competition and Innovation: A Case Study of the Mexican Road Freight Industry." Policy Research Working Paper No. 2318, World Bank, Washington, DC.

Dutz, M., J. Ordover, and R. Willig. 2000. "Entrepreneurship, Access Policy and Economic Development: Lessons from Industrial Organization." European Economic Review 44: 739–47.

European Commission. 2005. The Application of Competition Rules to Liner Shipping. Final report, Brussels, European Commission.

Federation of East and Southern African Road Transport Associations (FESARTA). 2007. "Chirundu One-Stop Border-Post Initiative Monitoring Project." Unpublished paper.

Fink, C., A. Mattoo, and I. C. Neagu. 2002. "Trade in International Maritime Services: How Much Does Policy Matter?" World Bank Economic Review 16 (1): 81–108.

Gesellschaft für Technische Zusammenarbeit (GTZ). 2007. "International Fuel Prices 2007." http://www.gtz.de/fuelprices.

Harding, I., G. Palsson, and G. Raballand. 2007. "Port and Maritime Transport Challenges in West and Central Africa." Sub-Saharan Africa Transport Policy Program SSATP Working Paper No. 84, World Bank, Washington, DC.

Limao, N., and A. J. Venables. 2001. "Infrastructure, Geographical Disadvantage and Transport Costs." World Bank Economic Review 15 (3): 451–79.

Londoño-Kent, P. 2007. "Road Freight Transport Industry in Low and Middle-Income Countries." Draft, World Bank, Washington, DC.

MacKellar, L., A. Wörgötter, and J. Wörz. 2002. "Economic Growth of Landlocked Countries." In Ökonomie in Theorie und Praxis, ed. G. Chaloupek, A. Guger, E. Nowotny, and G. Schwödiauer, 213–26. Berlin: Springer.

Mthembu-Salter, G. 2007. "The Cost of Nontariff Barriers to Business along the North-South Corridor (South Africa–Zimbabwe) via Beit Bridge: A Preliminary Study and Working Paper." South African Institute of International Affairs (SAIIA), Braamfontein, South Africa. http://saiia.org.za/images/upload/dttp_pap_mthembu-salter_ntb_20070827.pdf.

Mwase, N. 2003. "The Liberalisation, De-regulation and Privatisation of the Transport Sector in Sub-Saharan Africa: Experiences, Challenges and Opportunities." Journal of African Economies 12 (AERC Supplement 2): 153–92.

Oyer, S. 2007. "Freight Rates Determinants along the Northern Corridor Road." MSc Thesis, Nairobi UNES.

Pedersen, P. O. 2001. "Freight Transport under Globalization and Its Impact on Africa." *Journal of Transport Geography* 9: 85–99.

Raballand, G., C. Kunaka, and B. Giersing. 2007. "Effects of Regional Liberalization and Harmonization in Road Transport: A Focus on Zambia number and Lessons for Landlocked Countries." Policy Research Working Paper, World Bank, Washington, DC.

Rizet, C., and H. Gwet. 1998. "Transport de Marchandises: Une Comparaison Internationale des Prix du Camionnage—Afrique, Asie du Sud Est, Amérique Centrale." *Recherche–Transports–Sécurités* 60: 68–88.

Rizet, C., and J. Hine. 1993. "A Comparison of the Costs and Productivity of Road Freight Transport in Africa and Pakistan." *Transport Reviews* 13(2).

Snow, T., M. Faye, J. McArthur, and J. Sachs. 2003. "Country Case Studies on the Challenges Facing Landlocked Developing Countries." Background paper for HDR 2003. http://hdr.undp.org/en/reports/global/hdr2003/papers/landlocked_countries_2003.pdf.

Souley, H. 2001. "Dérèglementation du Transport Routier de Marchandises au Niger et Intégration Sous-Régionale." PhD Thesis, INRETS, Paris.

Tera International. 2005. "Malawi Transport Cost Study." Washington, DC.

United Nations Conference on Trade and Development (UNCTAD). 1975. *Code of Conduct for Liner Conferences*. http://www.unctad.org/ttl/legal.

World Bank. 1994. *Bank Lending for African Transport Corridors: An OED Review*. Washington, DC: World Bank.

———. 2004. *Reducing the Economic Distance to Market*. Washington, DC: World Bank.

———. 2005. *East Africa Trade and Transport Facilitation Project*. Washington, DC: World Bank.

———. 2006. *Review of Selected Railway Concessions in Sub-Saharan Africa*. Washington, DC: World Bank.

———. 2007a. *Agriculture in Sub-Saharan Africa. An Independent Evaluation Group Review of World Bank Assistance*. Washington, DC: World Bank.

———. 2007b. "Trade and Transport Facilitation in South Asia." Unpublished paper, World Bank, Washington, DC.

Bank Support for Africa Transport Corridors

The World Bank has supported transport corridors, in Africa and elsewhere, through two types of activities: (i) investment projects and analytical studies of corridors in individual countries, and (ii) research on trade and transport corridors.

World Bank support for transport corridors in Africa dates back to the 1970s. However, support during the early years was almost exclusively focused on improving infrastructure. A review of the African corridor projects by the World Bank's Independent Evaluation Group[1] found that most projects were limited in coverage to a single transport mode or agency and centered upon the development or rehabilitation of physical facilities. The projects were meant primarily to meet the infrastructure needs of the countries of project location. Project achievements with respect to corridor transit traffic proved to be minimal, mainly because of the projects' narrow focus on a single transport mode (therefore ignoring connectivity and operations; for example, between ports and roads), and because of the lack of emphasis on institutional reforms. This is not surprising and was actually necessary at the early stage of Africa development back in the 1970s–90s, when focus had to be at the national level of stability and accessibility. However, once the national level accesses and connections are basically established, the investment strategy should be expanded to include a subregional and regional dimension. A key conclusion of the report was that the World Bank needs to step up its support for corridor projects and studies and that prerequisites for future operations should be intercountry agreements on corridor operations, including access, maintenance, and streamlining and harmonization of regulation.

One of the most comprehensive World Bank operations in recent years has focused on trade and facilitation in East Africa. Currently the Bank has two investment projects of this type in the East and Central Africa corridor: one in the Western Africa corridor that recently was approved, and another project in the corridor between Abidjan and Lagos that is currently under preparation. Since 1995, the World Bank has supported several rail concessions in Africa, including two binational concessions (Senegal–Mali and Burkina–Côte d'Ivoire). An important lesson from these projects is that the impact of rail concession is more on the reliability of service and stronger competition with road operators than on an actual decrease of transport costs.

Note

1. World Bank (1994). This report covered 42 completed projects in 14 countries, including eight landlocked countries (Rwanda, Burundi, Malawi, Zambia, Central African Republic, Burkina Faso, and Mali) and six littoral countries (Kenya, Tanzania, Cameroon, Benin, Côte d'Ivoire, and Senegal).

Data Methodology and Reliability

1. Data Selection

The final database is composed by 192 observations along 11 routes including 10 international routes in 7 countries: Burkina Faso, Ghana, Cameroon, Chad, Uganda, Kenya, and Zambia. The selected corridors were chosen in terms of data reliability, route importance in terms of trade volume, and significant amount of observations available. Outliers have been excluded from the database.[1] In data selection few assumptions (mentioned below) were taken while preserving the original answers from the survey.

2. Variable Description

2.a. Transport Prices

2.a.i. Inputs

Distance: Distance measured in kilometers. Source: Distance charts available in the countries.

Payload utilization: Yearly mileage on empty haul for the route i / Yearly mileage ($i = 1;2;3;4;$ or 5 for trucking companies and $i = 1$ for truckers). Variable measured in kilometers.

Turnarounds: Number of turnarounds per year for a truck dedicated to this route.

Yearly mileage: Turnarounds * Distance. Variable measured in kilometers.

Average load: Average load in tons from origin to destination (base value for return trip).

Price per trip:

If [unit = Tons] [Price per unit * Average load]
If [unit = Container] [Price per unit]
If [unit = Liters] [Price per unit * Average load * 1000]
If [unit = Kilometers] [Price per unit * Average load * Distance]
Else [Price per unit * Average load * Distance]

Price per trip is measured originally in local currency (converted into current U.S. dollars using IMF exchange rates) for a standard load (container of truck load).

Assumption: Because of the lack of information about when the truck is empty we assume that:

If [Average route Price per trip to go >= Average route Price per trip return] [Price per trip = Price per trip to go]

Else [Price per trip = Price per trip return]

Principal product: Principal product transported[2] categorical variable.
Assumption: Because of the lack of information about when the truck is empty we assume that

If [Average route Price per trip to go >= Average route Price per trip return] [Principal product transported = Principal product transported to go]

Else [Principal product transported = Principal product transported return]

2.a.ii.   *Outputs*

Yearly revenue: Yearly revenue to go + Yearly revenue return. Revenue is measured in terms of full truckload equivalents.

Given the lack of information about when the truck is empty, we assume that if price discrepancies exist between the price to go and the price return, the truck is going full loaded one way and partly loaded the other way.[3] Therefore, payload utilization impact is attributed to the least profitable way, using the following formulas:

Yearly revenue to go:

If [Price per trip to go > Price per trip return] [Price per trip to go * Turnarounds]

If [Price per trip to go = Price per trip return] [Price per trip to go * Turnarounds * Payload utilization]

If [Price per trip to go < Price per trip return] [Price per trip to go * Turnarounds * (Payload utilization)* 2]

Yearly revenue return:

If [Price per trip to go < Price per trip return] [Price per trip to go * Turnarounds]

If [Price per trip to go = Price per trip return] [Price per trip to go * Turnarounds * Payload utilization]

If [Price per trip to go > Price per trip return] [Price per trip return * Turnarounds * (Payload utilization–0.5) * 2]

2.b.   Transport Costs

Fleet: New vehicles + Secondhand vehicles

Age: New vehicles * Average age of new vehicles + Secondhand vehicles * Average age of secondhand vehicles] / Fleet

2.b.i.   Fixed costs per day is the sum of staff costs, license costs, overhead costs, insurance costs, communication costs, security costs, losses, financial costs, and depreciation costs. All fixed costs are calculated as an average for a truck owned by the company (that is, Total costs divided by Fleet) and per calendar day (divided by 365). The original values are in local currency and were converted into current U.S. dollars using IMF exchange rates.

Staff: Cost of labor, including wages, salaries, and bonuses and social payments / Fleet

License: Cost of licenses / Fleet

Overhead: Overhead costs, including rental of land/buildings, equipment, and furniture and excluding all the other fixed costs / Fleet

Insurance: Insurance cost / Fleet

Communication: Cost of communication / Fleet

Security:
If [The establishment paid for security = Yes] [Total annual security cost / Fleet] or [Annual cost as percentage of total sales * Total sales / Fleet]
Else [0]

Losses:
If [The establishment experienced losses as a result of road accidents or theft and robbery = Yes] [Total annual losses / Fleet] or [Percentage of total sales * Total sales / Fleet]
Else [0]

Finance: Interest rates provided by the survey respondents are supposed to be actual annual percentage rates (APR) for truck purchases. Companies that do not have access to bank loans to finance their trucks (cash financing) are supposed to bear no financial costs.

If [Percentage of recent purchases financed by bank loan is all blank] [0] (i.e., the establishment has not bought trucks in the last 3 years and has therefore no bank loan to repay)
If [Percentage of recent purchases financed by bank loan is all null] [0] (i.e., the establishment does not finance its fixed assets through bank loans)
Else, [Percentage of bank loan finance purchace/100 * Interest rate/100 * Purchase price of the truck]

Depreciation: All companies bear depreciation costs. These costs are, however, inversely proportionate to the number of years of use and are therefore almost null for companies that use their truck for a large number of years. Some companies do not fully depreciate their new trucks and secondhand trucks and keep a good resale value. We have modeled the resale value drop of an average new truck owned by the establishment by the following formula:

Drop new = minimum(logarithm(Years of use / 4 * (exponential (0,5)–1)+1);1) and the resale value drop of an average secondhand truck owned by the establishment by the formula value:

Drop secondhand = minimum(logarithm(Years of use / 5 * (exponential (0,5)–1)+1);1).

The main assumption here is the logarithmic drop of the truck resale value, with an estimated residual value of 50 percent reached after 4 years for new trucks and 5 years for secondhand trucks. After 11 years and 14 years, respectively, for new and secondhand trucks, the residual value would be null. The periods have been extrapolated from local interviews of transport companies. As for the purchase value, we use the value provided by the person interviewed or a default value when data were not provided. We differentiated between years of use on the road for new trucks and years of use on the road for secondhand trucks.

Depreciation costs = (Depreciation costs new + Depreciation costs secondhand) / Fleet

If [New vehicles > 0] [Depreciation costs new = New truck purchase value * New vehicles * minimum[Drop new; 100 percent] / Years of use]
Else [0]

If [Secondhand vehicles > 0] [Depreciation costs secondhand = Secondhand truck purchase value * Secondhand vehicles * minimum [Drop secondhand; 100 percent] / Years of use]
Else [0]

2.b.ii.   *Variable costs* per kilometer is the sum of fuel costs, tire costs, maintenance costs, and bribes. Variable costs are route specific ($i = 1; 2; 3; 4;$ or 5). Survey data, however, do not relate variable costs to routes traveled (except for bribes), and we assume that fuel and tire consumption and maintenance costs are uniform within the company fleet. The original values are in local currency and were converted into current U.S. dollars using IMF exchange rates.

Fuel: Companies have provided the average fuel consumption of light-weight, mediumweight, and heavyweight trucks. The tonnage ranges used in the questionnaire are, respectively, 0–5 tons for light weight, 5–7 tons for medium weight, and 7+ for heavy weight. However, feedback from interviewers has encouraged us to use different ranges: 0–10 tons, 10–20 tons, and 20–30 tons, respectively, because these are more representative of actual loads.

The unit fuel cost (LCU per liter) has been derived from "International Fuel Prices (2007), 5th edition data preview, GTZ (2006 values) using the IMF-IFS exchange rates (Q4 2006). We have used the super gasoline price (3 to 10 percent higher than the diesel price in the countries selected) as an estimate of the fuel plus lubricant unit cost (no relevant source of lubricant cost available).

For trucking companies, fuel cost per km is:

If [Actual load <= 10] [Fuel consumption light weight/100 * Unit fuel cost]
If [10 > Actual load >= 20] [Fuel consumption medium weight/100 * Unit fuel cost]
If [Actual load > 20] [Fuel consumption heavy weight/100 * Unit fuel cost]

For truckers, fuel cost per km is calculated using the same formula as for trucking companies but using systematically the default value for fuel consumption because average consumption data is not available.

Tires: The questionnaire provides us with extensive data on the companies, and truckers' new tire, secondhand tire, and retread tire consumption. The unit tire cost is not always provided, and the category average in the country is used as default value. We assume that trucks use an average 12 tires and the distribution of new, secondhand, and retread tires is homogeneous in the establishment's truck fleet.

Tire cost per km= 12 * [percentage of new * Cost of New / Life of new + percentage of secondhand * Cost of secondhand / Life of secondhand + percentage of retread * Cost of Retread / Life of retread]. Where unit cost or average life in km was not provided we used the default value.

Maintenance: Annual maintenance costs per km are provided by trucking companies for each truck category:

For trucking industry Maintenance = Annual maintenance costs (or default value) / Yearly mileage

For truckers, Maintenance = Cost of servicing, repairs, spare parts, excluding fuel tires and lubricants / (Fleet * Yearly mileage). We assume yearly mileage is homogeneous within the same truckers' fleet.

Bribes: Bribe paid on the selected route / Distance

2.b.iii.   Fixed–variable cost ratio:
[(Fixed Cost per day * 365/ Turnarounds) / (Fixed Cost per day * 365 / Turnarounds + Variable cost per km * 2 * Distance] percent -
[(Variable cost per km * 2 * Distance) / (Fixed Cost per day * 365 / Turnarounds + Variable cost per km * 2 * Distance] percent

Note about default value. When data were not available, we calculated a default value as the average of available data on that variable.

Note about the sources. With the exception of Distance, Unit fuel cost, and the exchange rates, all the data are coming from the trucking survey.

2.c.   Profitability

Profit margin per turnaround:
(Yearly revenue / Turnarounds) / (2 * Variable costs * Distance + Fixed costs * 365 / Turnarounds) − 1

2.d.   Quality Indexes

2.d.i. Transport quality: This infrastructure quality index by country has been calculated as a weighted average of other indexes using the following weights:

Parameters	Weighting coefficients
Education	2
Experience	1
Domestic competition	2
Contracts	2
Tracking system	1
Fleet	1
Age	3
Number of employees	1

Education: Weighted average[4] of the highest level of education of the top manager.

Experience: Average of years of managerial experience working in this sector of the top manager.

Domestic competition: Weighted average[5] of the importance of the pressure from domestic transporters on reducing operating costs of existing transport services or expanding services.

Contracts: Average of the percentage of all the freight business obtained through contracts with clients.

Tracking system: Percentage of companies with a communication tracking system.

Number of employees: Average amount of full-time employees including managers, truck drivers, and mechanics (service/repair).

Note about the transport quality index. All fields have been normalized between 0 and 1. The index is calculated considering absolute averages for education, experience, domestic competition, and contracts; and relative indices with respect to the country maximum value as reference for tracking system, fleet age, and number of employees.

Note about the source. The data come from the trucking survey.

2.d.ii.   Negotiation power: Average of the sum of the percentage of all the freight businesses for which price is determined by negotiating with clients. Freight business could be obtained by independent freight agents, through public-private institutions in charge of freight allocation, by telephone/fax from customers, by trucks waiting at lorry parks, by drivers finding their own loads, and through contract with clients. Index normalized between 0 and 1.

2.d.iii.   Logistic perception index (LPI): The LPI is a set of indicators that measure perceptions of the logistics environment of 140 countries on several logistics dimensions (such as transport cost, infrastructure, customs, and so forth). The survey uses an anonymous, Web-based questionnaire that asks respondents to evaluate their country of residence, as well as eight countries they are dealing with, on several logistics dimensions:

- International transportation costs
- Domestic transportation costs
- Timeliness of shipments
- Tractability of shipments
- Transport and IT infrastructure
- Customs and other border procedures
- Logistics competence

Source: Global facilitation partnership for transportation and trade.

2.d.iv.   Infrastructure condition: This index measures the percentage of the road section in good and fair condition. Index normalized between 0 and 1. *Source*: Africa transport unit.

2.e.   Other Variables

Rail competition: Categorical variable[6] that represents the level of obstacle that rail competition represents to the current transport operations of the establishment.

Taxes: Taxes paid on the establishment / Fleet. The original values are in local currency.

Number of borders: Number of borders crossed by the truck (route specific variable).

Region: Regional[7] dummy variable.

3.   Regression Analysis

3.a.   Regression Variables

In the regression analysis, the variables are measured in current U.S. dollars per kilometer per truck. The original variables were recalculated as

Prices per km: Price per trip / Distance

Fixed costs per km: Fixed costs * 365 / (Distance * Turnarounds)
Variable costs per km: Variable costs

3.b. Data Reliability

Variables	Data reliability
Prices	Reliable
Fixed costs	
Staff costs	Reliable/dubious
License costs	Reliable/dubious
Overhead costs	Reliable/dubious
Insurance costs	Reliable/dubious
Communication costs	Dubious/unreliable
Security costs	Reliable/dubious
Loses costs	Reliable/dubious
Finance costs	Reliable
Depreciation costs	Reliable/dubious
Variable costs	
Fuel costs	Reliable/dubious
Maintenance costs	Dubious/unreliable
Tire costs	Reliable/dubious
Bribes	Reliable/dubious
Others	
Distance	Unreliable
Number of turnarounds	Reliable
Payload utilization	Dubious
Taxes	Dubious/unreliable

Notes

1. Nine outliers with respect to prices or costs were omitted from the database (two observations in Cameroon, four observations in Chad, two observations in Ghana, and one observation in Kenya). An extreme example comes from the Nairobi–Eldoret route: the observation excluded was more than 8,500 percent smaller than the average price value and 8,200 percent smaller than the smallest value considered in the average.

2. Principal product transported is classified as oil-related products, food imports, agricultural exports, general goods, production inputs, equipment, and empty.

3. Total payload utilization = (Payload utilization to go + Payload utilization return)/2.

4. The weights are MBA (3), other postgraduate degree (PhD, Master's) (2.5), graduate degree (2), vocational training or some university training (1), secondary school (0.75), primary school (0.5), and no education (0).

5. The weights are very important (1), fairly important (2/3), slightly important (1/3).

6. Levels of obstacle are classified as no obstacle, minor, moderate, major, and very severe obstacle.

7. West Africa: Ghana, Burkina Faso; Central Africa: Cameroon, Chad; East Africa: Kenya, Uganda; Southern Africa: Zambia.

Sample Survey Design and Data Quality Control

An Example with Cameroon

Survey Coverage

The Trucking Survey in Cameroon targeted trucking companies and companies conducting their own transportation. A trucking company is defined as a company that conducts trucking as its main operation and that has five or more full-time paid employees. The companies surveyed serve at least one of the following routes:

- Douala–Yaoundé
- Douala–Ngaoundéré
- Douala–N'Djaména
- Douala–Bangui
- Douala–Bertoua
- Douala–Garoua Boulai
- Douala–Bafoussam
- Yaoundé–Bafoussam

The survey also sampled a selection of truckers (trucking operators with fewer than five full-time permanent paid employees) that serve the main roads listed above.

Companies with Five or More Full-Time Paid Permanent Employees

A list of Cameroonian trucking operators was obtained from the World Bank Transport Unit. This list was completed and updated during the early stages of the survey. To validate the list and to classify the establishments according to size, the EEC team tried to contact a selection of establishments drawn randomly from the list. Following the results of the validation process, a sample frame consisting of a population of 52 establishments was set.

An attempt was made to contact each of these establishments. During the survey, it was discovered that 10 establishments were closed, 8 establishments were unreachable despite repeated attempts by phone, 12 establishments refused to participate, and 22 establishments agreed to participate, resulting in 22 completed trucking questionnaires, of which 5 companies provided their own transportation.

Truckers

In this survey, the trucker's stratum covers all establishments of the trucking industry with fewer than five employees. For many reasons, including the small size of establishments, their expected high rate of turnovers, the high level of "informality" of establishments, and consequently the difficulty in obtaining trustworthy information from official sources, the survey firm selected an aerial sampling approach to estimate the population of establishments and select the sample in this stratum according to the roads to be covered.

First, to randomly select individual truckers establishments for surveying, the following procedure was followed: (i) select districts and specific zones of each district where there are lorry parks or where truckers usually off-load; (ii) count all truckers who generally stop in these specific lorry parks; (iii) in accordance with this count, create a virtual list and select establishments at random from that virtual list; and (iv) on the basis of the ratio between the number selected in each specific zone and the total population in that zone, create and apply a skip rule for selecting establishments in that zone.

The survey firm went into the field to count truckers in the selected areas. Once the count for each zone was completed, the numbers were sent back to the firm headquarters.

At head office the following procedure was followed: the count by zone was converted into a list of sequential numbers for the entire survey region, and a computer program performed a random selection of the determined number of establishments from the list. Then, depending on the number that the computer selected in each specific zone, a skip rule was defined to select truckers to survey in that zone. The skip rule for each zone was sent back to the field team.

In Cameroon, enumerators were sent to each zone with instructions as to how to apply the skip rule defined for that zone as well as how to select replacements in the event of a refusal or other cause of nonparticipation (see table A3.1 below).

Data Quality Control

A management policy for the interviewers was established, and the following procedures were applied during the execution of the survey:

(A) Daily meetings with each interviewer at the end of the day for the first revision of their questionnaire(s). The objectives of this first pass through the questionnaire were

    (1) To verify that all of the questions had been answered and that basic constraints had been respected. If the questionnaire failed this aspect of the review badly, it was returned to the enumerator to complete (through a return visit if necessary). The basic checks here included

Table A3.1   Survey Participation by Country

Country	Companies	Approached	Closed	Refused	Unavailable	Surveyed	Actual
Burkina	Trucking						
Faso	companies	—	—	—	—	18	**16**
	Truckers	—	—	—	—	45	**45**
Ghana	Trucking						
	companies	35	4	6	7	18	**15**
	Truckers	110	0	30	25	55	**54**
Cameroon	Trucking						
	companies	52	10	12	8	22	**14**
	Truckers	120	0	40	23	57	**57**
Chad	Trucking						
	companies	34	0	8	8	18	**14**
	Truckers	135	0	50	28	57	**57**
Kenya	Trucking						
	companies	64	1	2	1	22	**21**
	Truckers	—	—	—	—	—	**55**
Uganda	Trucking						
	companies	47	4	8	14	21	**17**
	Truckers	100	0	20	23	57	**57**
Zambia	Trucking						
	companies	50	4	20	1	1	**19**
	Truckers	—	—	—	—	—	**45**

Source: Trucking survey.
Note: No available data for Burkina Faso.

(a) that no fields had been left empty (other than explicitly skipped fields),

(b) that no fields had been filled in ambiguously (that is, with a dash, slash, or squiggle),

(c) that coded responses of DK (don't know), NA (not applicable), and R (refused to answer) seemed plausible for the field in question,

(d) that percentages, where required, added up to 100 percent, and

(e) that fields with known relationships to adjacent fields respected those relationships (for example, the year of manufacturing a vehicle is smaller than the year of purchasing that vehicle).

(2) To take the opportunity to reinforce the enumerators' awareness of the logical links between questions, by quickly checking the more obvious ones, demonstrating what they are doing, highlighting any inconsistencies, and asking for explanations. Some of the consistency checks that might be done quickly at this stage included:

(a) if the establishment did or did not perform cross-border operations (that is, yes or no but not NA), in which case the main point of exit that the establishment used should be listed;

(b) if the establishment owned lightweight vehicles, it should have the total cost of maintenance and the average fuel consumption for this type of vehicle;

(c) if there are some trips with overload fines in certain routes they should have the amount of overload fines per trip.

(3) To ensure that the full consistency checks were carried out using an SPSS script after the data had been entered, and reviewed in a second meeting with the enumerator (see C below).

(4) To assess the interviewer's ability to correctly fill out the questionnaire and to clarify any concerns regarding his understanding of the questionnaire, if necessary.

(B) Following this review, the questionnaire was retained by the firm survey for data entry and the administration of coherence tests, unless it badly failed the first basic tests listed in A(1) above. Within a short time frame (one or two days after the first meeting), the questionnaire was entered, and the coherence and completion tests for each questionnaire were executed.

(C) There was a second meeting with the interviewer in order to go over the results of the coherence and completion tests and, if necessary, return the questionnaire for further completion/verification.

(D) Data entry and consistency checks

  (1) When data entry was finished for the day, for each type of questionnaire for which additional cases were entered or existing cases were updated, that data files were exported to SPSS format.

  (2) The resulting SPSS script was run to open the data in SPSS.

  (3) The consistency and completion tests scripts were run in order to generate data regarding the completion status of each case and to validate the consistency checks. This procedure generated a report detailing these results as well as the completion status of the whole sample with respect to sales.

  (4) Whenever possible, this report was printed and reviewed with the enumerators and possible return visits were executed if required shortly thereafter.

(E) Completion tests

A questionnaire was considered "final" when it contained answers to 85 percent of the questions in each section. In addition, across the entire set of completed questionnaires, each variable was submitted to an 85 percent completion test. Finally, all information pertaining to the screener portion of the questionnaire had to be completed.

Sample Size

The number of vehicles surveyed and details about those vehicles are shown in table A3.2.

Table A3.2   Number of Vehicles Surveyed by Country

Country	Companies	Light weight (<5 tons)	Medium weight (>=5–7 tons)	Heavy weight (> 7 tons)	Total
Burkina Faso	Trucking companies	4	22	216	**242**
	Truckers	3	17	117	**137**
Ghana	Trucking companies	0	1	298	**299**
	Truckers	2	12	77	**91**
Cameroon	Trucking companies	15	10	389	**414**
	Truckers	14	32	42	**88**
Chad	Trucking companies	0	0	290	**290**
	Truckers	0	1	66	**67**
Kenya	Trucking companies	20	67	1,096	**1,183**
	Truckers	0	15	122	**137**
Uganda	Trucking companies	104	66	240	**410**
	Truckers	2	16	72	**90**
Zambia	Trucking companies	66	109	495	**670**
	Truckers	32	32	29	**93**

Source: Trucking survey.
Note: Each weight category includes trucks, trailers, and semitrailers. Tractors and towing vehicles are not included.

Freight Allocation through Freight Bureaus: The Cases of Central and West Africa

The strong regulation of transport activities is probably the most distinctive feature of the Central African corridors. Transit is governed by transit agreements signed between the governments of Cameroon and Chad, on the one hand, and the governments of Cameroon and the Central African Republic, on the other hand. Apart from banning cabotage, these agreements signed in 1999 set the principles of traffic allocation between fleets of coastal and landlocked countries: 65 percent of freight through Cameroon has to be allocated to Chadian freight operators and 60 percent to Central African freight operators.

Three national institutions, called freight bureaus, are responsible for the implementation of these agreements' provisions:

- for Cameroon, the Bureau de Gestion du Fret Terrestre (BGFT)
- for Chad, Bureau National de Fret (BNF)
- for the Central African Republic, the Bureau d'Affrètement Routier Centrafricain (BARC)

Although they have different legal status, their objectives are similar:

- to collect and publish offers and demand for transport
- to manage the issuance of cargo and transit-related documents

- to ensure, on behalf of their country, that the freight quotas are respected
- to monitor the movement of goods overland and to keep statistics related to goods transport

The BGFT also organizes the transit operations and oversees procedural and transit facilitation issues from Douala and Ngaoundéré. In theory, the three structures act as arbitrators to balance the differences in quota implementation and ensure that small operators have the same access to cargo as larger ones. Their regulatory role is normally limited to quota oversight, but they also define reference freight rates that in practice set the actual rates charged by transporters.

In reality, to get a load, truck drivers have to be registered on the BGFT directory and wait in a parking lot at the exit of the Douala (or in the equivalent parking lots in Ngaoundéré and Belabo). The transaction is negotiated separately between the importer and the truck owner. This negotiation is theoretically a free negotiation between the transporter and the importer agent. However, the "market price," extremely high and very uniform between operators, clearly shows that the importer's negotiation power is nonexistent.

Long-term contracting is nonexistent in the subregion. Getting a load depends on the issuance of transport documents from the BGFT and BNF or BARC. Consequently, if a shipper/transporter wishes to bypass the freight bureaus, transport documents are not issued and then the transporter/shipper takes a high risk of problems with the controlling agencies.

West Africa's regulatory environment is similar to that of Central Africa. Bilateral treaties are in place because after a crisis that followed the 1992 transport deregulation, the government of Burkina Faso signed an agreement with all its corridor partners (Ghana, Côte d'Ivoire, Togo, and Benin) to establish quotas: one third for transit country truckers and two thirds for the Burkinabé truckers. The CBC (Conseil Burkinabé des Chargeurs) has the responsibility of ensuring that this rule is enforced. Its agents in each port deliver transport authorization for each load. In theory, as in Central Africa, freight allocation is the result of a free and independent bargain between the shipper and the trucker. The CBC registers the result of this business transaction with no involvement whatsoever. It only enforces the one-third/two-third rule when necessary.[1]

In practice, the CBC has been put in a unique monopolistic position that allows it to control the market. It is de facto a freight allocation bureau that distributes loads between trucking companies with the active support of the main trucking company association, OTRAF (Organisation des Transporteurs du Faso). OTRAF is the only transporters' association in the country. It was created in 1995 with the active support of the government and the chamber of commerce to be a unique interlocutor rather than the then four competing associations. However, OTRAF was in a monopolistic position that was rapidly captured by some well-connected individuals. As a result, competing associations soon reemerged but so far have not managed to successfully compete with OTRAF.

The unofficial rules in a port in West Africa are as follows:

- A shipper informs the CBC it has a shipment to be transported to Burkina Faso.
- The CBC then informs the OTRAF about this shipment and all its details. It may or may not negotiate the tariff with the shipper.
- OTRAF turns to its constituents and assigns the load on a first come–first served basis. This *tour de rôle* is updated in real time: when a truck arrives in the port, the driver goes to the OTRAF representative to be added to the waiting list.
- Once the contract is established, the trucker pays its due to the association (FCFA 10,000) for the service it provided and to the CBC (FCFA 10,200) for the loading authorization.[2]

Notes

1. To make sure that the whole trade flows are accounted for, no shipper has the right to be its own trucker: no own-account trucking is allowed from the port, although exceptions are granted by the administration on a case-by-case basis.
2. Such costs are close to 10 times higher in Central Africa.

Zambia's Road Freight Industry and Business Practices in Southern Africa

Zambia's road freight industry faces competition from other Southern African operators. Several foreign trucking companies operate extensively along Zambian main transport corridors. The importance of foreign operators can be seen in table A5.1, which gives the estimated[1] numbers of trucks that operate on a continuous basis on the different routes and that are registered in other SADC countries. The market is therefore highly competitive, but Zambian trucking companies' market share is close to 40 percent, which is more than the "real" market share of landlocked countries in other regulated systems.

The number of foreign trucks operating in Zambia is high because Zambia is a net exporter in terms of freight volumes. Consequently, this makes it economically viable for South African companies to undertake turnaround trips. The South African fleet is the most important in the subregion, benefiting from economies of scale. The Gauteng heavy truck fleet is about eight times larger than the Zambian fleet.[2] Thus, some large South African trucking companies have taken over control of several large Zambian companies, which is also a specificity of Zambian trucking industry. Foreign direct investment in the trucking industry has been the main solution South African companies found to bypass market/entry barriers. However, it is worth noting that although some large companies benefit from South African capital, they are run by Zambian management.

Table A5.1 Indicative Cost Factor Ranges for Zambia and South Africa Trucking Companies Operating to and from Zambia

Cost factor	Zambia	South Africa
Truck acquisition		
Used trucks	Used trucks—purchase from Europe or America. No government incentives to renew fleet.	Used—purchased on domestic market. Levels of utilization would not be able to meet costs of new truck.
Financing	Self-financing, informal borrowing, local interest rates said to be high.	Local banks, but finance charges are high (17 percent).
Lifespan	8–10 years	5–10 years
Trailers	Bought locally or South Africa.	Bought locally.
Spares and tires	Keep in-house stock, bought directly from suppliers. Borrowed financing.	Limited in-house stock for routine maintenance needs. Other spares readily available on local market.
Average annual mileage range	96–108,000 km per year (one company reported as high as 120,000 km per year). Vehicles make 2–2.5 trips per month.	96–108,000 km per year for cross border and up to 240,000 km per year for domestic operations. Vehicles make 2–2.5 trips per month.

Fuel costs (2007)	US$1.50 per liter	US$0.88 per liter
Turnaround time	8–12 days	7–14 days
Downtime because of breakdown	Minimal, but total downtime including maintenance can be up to 20 percent of the time.	1–2 percent of the transport time, stringent maintenance regimes.
Empty running	0–5 percent, better able to secure export traffic, which is thinner so minimizes empty running.	0–5 percent, agents in each country.
Weighbridges	Roads authority, spend on average three hours waiting. Offload if overloaded, driver and transporter fined.	In-house, municipal for self regulation. Offload if overloaded, driver and transporter fined.
Labor	Shortage of well-trained drivers. Bonus for drivers.	Not an issue. Drivers paid mileage bonus.
Rates	Rates determined by RSA operators.	Fro example: R 28,396 for Johannesburg–Copperbelt (approx. US$4,028) for a 34 ton payload, or approx. US$118 per ton. Range is US$90–170 per ton. Export rates can be 60–100 percent of import rate.

In terms of freight rate determination, once the agents are approached by a shipper, they obtain quotes from trucking companies and negotiate a rate within the limits set by the shipper with an allowance for the agents' own margin. The large agents insist that they work with reputable and large transport companies so they are better able to deliver a reliable service. The agents, who deal mainly with import traffic, prefer to use South African trucking companies.

Despite the existence of a competitive shipping agents sector, some of the trucking companies are increasingly entering into direct contracts with the shippers. As a result of the trend toward direct contracting, shipping agents have to adapt and offer more comprehensive logistics services.

Contrary to widespread trends in West and Central Africa, and to a lesser extent East Africa, axle load regulation is widely enforced. That is what was concluded from the results of an independent axle load benchmark test carried out in October–November 2006 in Zambia. At a mobile weighbridge located just before the Kafue Weighbridge Station coming from Chirundu, only 4.22 percent of the tested vehicles were loaded with more than 5 percent of the gross vehicle mass (compared with 7 percent in 2005). At Kapiri Mposhi, only 4.33 percent of vehicles passing through the mobile weighbridge were overloaded, down from 35 percent in the previous test. This is attributed to strict enforcement by the authorities and also to the fact that all the operators were consulted, especially the transporters.

Notes

1. The statistics provided by the cross-border agencies in Zambia and South Africa, and also the Zambian Revenue Authority, do not included data on the number of trucks using the various road corridors. The only effective way to obtain this information would be to undertake a detailed border-post and customs survey. Temporary permits do not indicate the numbers of trips carried out by each truck for the duration of the permit. Estimates are based on data from cross-border permits, customs records, previous observations of border posts, and information provided by selected transport providers.

2. Gauteng represents 38 percent of South Africa's vehicles, but more likely about 50 percent of the registered heavy trucks in South Africa.

Index

Page numbers followed by n. and a number refer to numbered notes. Page numbers followed by t or f refer to tables or figures, respectively. Page numbers in italic refer to boxed text.

ECO-AUDIT
Environmental Benefits Statement

The World Bank is committed to preserving endangered forests and natural resources. The Office of the Publisher has chosen to print *Transport Prices and Costs in Africa: A Review of the Main International Corridors* on recycled paper with 30 percent post consumer fiber, in accordance with the recommended standards for paper usage set by the Green Press Initiative, a nonprofit program supporting publishers in using fiber that is not sourced from endangered forests. For more information, visit www.greenpressinitiative. org.

Saved:
- 4 trees
- 20 million BTUs of total energy
- 3,002 lbs. of net green-house gases
- 9,763 gallons of waste water
- 1,152 lb. of solid waste

green
press
INITIATIVE

www.ingramcontent.com/pod-product-compliance
Lightning Source LLC
Chambersburg PA
CBHW061743270326
41928CB00011B/2359